The Supreme Court in the Political Process

Samuel Krislov

University of Minnesota

The Macmillan Company, New York
Collier–Macmillan Limited, London

Contents

CHAPTER 1

Recruitment: Judges

A. Criteria for Selection

LESS THAN 100 men have sat upon the Supreme Court bench. In 1963, at the time of President Kennedy's death, 94 out of the 118 men whose names had been submitted by Presidents to the Senate had actually been confirmed and had served as associate justices. About 300 men have served as circuit court or court of appeals judges, and approximately 1,225 have served on federal district courts.

These are small numbers compared to the opportunities available in other kinds of governmental service. Federal judgeship is regarded as the capstone of a career for even a very distinguished lawyer or public servant. Appointment to the Supreme Court is an honor second perhaps only to election as President of the United States. And others besides William Howard Taft, the only man to serve as both President and Chief Justice of the United States, hold the latter office to be the greater honor. Public opinion surveys have repeatedly shown that "Supreme Court Justice" has to the American citizen the highest status of any occupation.

The high standing of the office is one of the fundamental facts about federal judgeships. Supreme Court positions in particular are keenly sought after, and there is hard in-fighting for appointment to them; propriety and the fiction that a judgeship is a "calling" for which one waits passively mitigate the rigors of the behind-the-scenes campaign. Only a few men in each generation prove astute enough, powerful enough, and lucky enough to achieve this goal.

Who are they, these chosen ones, and how do they achieve their position? That bitterest of all satirists, Jonathan Swift, thought he knew the answer. Judges, he explained, were drawn from the fattest, laziest, and most corrupt of lawyers who wished to retire from the risks involved in living upon their fees. Their devotion to fraud was such, he reported, that he had "known several to refuse a bribe from the side where justice lay" so that they might decide in accordance with traditional legal oppressiveness.[1] This rare and mordant bit of cynicism hardly represents the general respect for the members of the bench, but it does reflect a strong streak of lay antipathy toward the legal profession generally and suggests some public doubts about the monopoly of high positions that lawyers hold in the legal order.

The specific monopoly that lawyers enjoy over federal judgeships rests upon the same public opinion that, on occasion, emotionally attacks it. There is no provision either in the Constitution or in statute that requires judges to have a legal background. Yet no President has ever seriously considered appointing anyone but lawyers to the bench. Even in 1937, at the height of the Court controversy, seven out of ten of those who had an opinion in a Gallup Poll on the question of nonlawyers for the Court opposed such a development.[2] Although the Supreme Court deals with an increasingly greater variety of considerations other than those of private and commercial law, which are the forte of the average attorney, there is still much which does require legal skills, though perhaps less than might be expected. That great legalist Cardozo found the type of political problem that came before the Supreme Court dull and uninteresting, and he longed for his days on the New York Court of Appeals when he could deal with what he regarded as "real" law.

But the monopoly of lawyers persists. It is significant because of the background, experience, and education that a lawyer is likely to have; it is significant because of the form in which discussion of issues before the courts will therefore continue to be cast; it is important also because it is part of a pattern of monopoly of key positions in the whole of the American government by lawyers.[3]

Such a monopoly is to be found in law enforcement offices scattered throughout our governmental system—prosecuting attorneys, U.S. district attorneys, attorneys general of the states, and the Attorney General of the United States. These offices constitute probably the single most developed and recognized career route for political figures in the United States. Crowned as this route is by judicial positions of tremendous power and prestige and ultimately by the Supreme Court, it is a durable channel, not only for the re-

---

[1] Jonathan Swift, *Gulliver's Travels.*

[2] AIPO Poll, March 1, 1937, reported in H. Cantril and M. Strunk, *Public Opinion 1935–1946* (Princeton: Princeton University Press, 1951), p. 388.

[3] See Joseph Schlesinger, "Lawyers and American Politics: A Clarified View," 1 *Midwest Journal of Political Science* (May 1957), pp. 26–39.

cruitment and training of officials who go on to the Court but also for those who move up the purely political ladder.

At the same time the inaccessibility of these offices to laymen represents at once a discouragement to political careers, the absence of a haven to escape to at stormy points in political careers, and an implicit—often explicit—handicap in standing and prestige. The inevitable question thrust at a witness before a congressional committee, "Are you a lawyer, Mr. Blank?" is part and parcel of this pattern of American politics.

But legal education and a lawyer's degree are not the only characteristics that Supreme Court justices have in common. A study of their careers and backgrounds shows that they are overwhelmingly of middle- and upper-class status. In the early years they were drawn largely from the gentry class, but even in recent times the older and more established middle-class groups have been disproportionately represented. Half of the remainder—one third of the total—have come from families that were politically active although not judicial. Only ten came from families of humble origin. Twelve justices were sons of prominent judges. Six married the daughters of judges, and an additional fifteen were related in some way to prominent jurists. Thus over a third were related to jurists and intimately connected with families "possessing the tradition of judicial service." [4] This recurrence of family names in the Court was highlighted most dramatically by the accession to the Court in 1955 of John Marshall Harlan, whose grandfather and namesake had been on the Court. This was rivaled by the presence on the same bench for nearly a decade of uncle and nephew, Justices Field and Brewer. Similarly, President Grover Cleveland nominated brothers to the Court in successive years, though as a result of the exigencies of politics Rufus Peckham was seated while Wheeler Peckham was rejected by the Senate.

Almost all the justices of the Supreme Court have been native-born; three out of the six foreign-born were appointed by George Washington. Yet the percentage of justices born abroad is higher than that of foreign-born congressmen. The members of the Supreme Court have been overwhelmingly of northwestern European stock, with English, Welsh, Scotch, and Irish constituting 88 per cent of the appointees. The remainder were of French, Dutch, Norwegian,

[4] John R. Schmidhauser, *The Supreme Court: Its Politics, Personalities and Procedures* (New York: Holt, 1960), pp. 34ff.

Germanic, and Iberian derivation. Italians and the large Slavic groups and nonwhites have never been represented.

But these percentages suggest a degree of nonrepresentativeness that is misleading. In the early period, of course, the ethnic stocks represented on the Court were in fact numerically dominant in the general population also. We have no reliable method of encapsulating ethnic distribution throughout our history. The time lag in the progress of an ethnic group from immigration to development of lawyers of prominence and ability is in part reflected in these figures as well. The predominance of the traditional stocks is as striking on the Supreme Court as it has been in the Presidency. On the other hand, the great religious groups of the country were represented much earlier on the Court than might have been expected. Chief Justice Taney was the first Catholic to serve; Chief Justice White, nearly sixty years later, was the second. In 1853 Millard Fillmore offered a Supreme Court appointment to Judah Benjamin of Louisiana; when Benjamin refused in order to take a seat in the United States Senate he left the distinction of becoming the first Jewish Supreme Court justice to Louis Brandeis in 1916.

The initial appointments of men of divergent faiths were in no way a recognition of any need for representation along religious lines. Nevertheless, with subsequent appointments like the choice of Frank Murphy to replace Butler, Frankfurter to replace Cardozo, and Goldberg to replace Frankfurter, the custom became institutionalized. There was a distinct feeling that appropriate positions on the Court were compensations for conspicuous disabilities in the political arena, notably with regard to the Presidency. An analogous custom prior to the election of President Kennedy was the Democratic party's preference where possible for a Catholic national chairman. Little attention seems to be given to sectarian differentiations among the various Protestant groups at the Supreme Court level. On the other hand, at the district court level and circuit court level there is a tendency for the predominant religious group in the area to be more strongly represented, even above its proportion in the population. At the Supreme Court level denominations with high social status—Episcopal, Presbyterian, Congregational, and Unitarian—have provided a substantial majority of all justices.

Presidents have chosen nearly all justices, and indeed all federal judges, from the membership of their own party. Since the posts are keenly sought after, and since individuals are seldom so pre-eminent that the President feels compelled to appoint any specific person, it is easy, with no great loss of equanimity, for him to insist upon finding the nominees among the ranks of his own political faith. Of the relatively few exceptions to this rule, like Eisenhower's choice of Brennan, a number were motivated by immediate political advantage. Hoover's choice of Cardozo was virtually thrust upon him. Cardozo was not only a Democrat but a New Yorker, the third on the Court, yet the pressure to appoint this distinguished jurist carried the day. Justice Stone went so far as to offer to resign from the Court in order to eliminate the overrepresentation of New York. William Howard Taft, who cared more about the ideology than the politics of prospective nominees, did appoint a Democrat (and a personal friend), Lurton, to the office; though Theodore Roosevelt had considered Lurton, he chose not to appoint him, probably in response to Senator Henry Cabot Lodge's argument: "I do not see why Republicans cannot be found who hold these opinions as well as Democrats." [5]

But though opinion does indeed count very heavily with Presidents, considerations of friendship are not unimportant. Justice Burton, a Republican and a conservative, was appointed by Truman at least in part on the basis of their previous association in the Senate, and also because Truman felt that some Republicans were necessary on an overwhelmingly Democratic bench. Occasionally difficult Cabinet members may even be "kicked upstairs" to the Court, which is rumored to have been the case with McLean and McReynolds. But in general, friendship with the President is a key variable. At least one writer who has thoroughly studied Court appointments concludes it is *the* key.[6]

Basically, however, the tendency of Presidents has been to reinforce the views that they would themselves espouse if they were on the Court. Even the effort to ascertain views can be complex, for as Lincoln wrote at one time, "We cannot ask a man what he will do, and if we should and he should answer us, we should despise him." [7] Direct examination about pending issues is deemed contrary to the notion of the proper role of the judge, who should approach the matter without promises and commitments, and inquiry must thus be made in a more roundabout fashion. Presidents have been aware of

[5] Lodge to Roosevelt, September 10, 1906, *Selections from the Correspondence of Henry Cabot Lodge* (New York: Scribner, 1925), II, p. 228.

[6] R. K. Burke, "The Path to the Court," Ph.D. Dissertation, Vanderbilt University, 1958 (University Microfilms), pp. 243–44.

[7] George S. Boutwell, *Reminiscences of Sixty Years in Public Affairs* (New York: McClure, Philips & Co., 1902), II, p. 29.

their responsibility, bearing in mind the maxim that "The good that Presidents do is interred with their bones. Their Supreme Court appointments live on after them." In a famous exchange with Henry Cabot Lodge, President Theodore Roosevelt inquired about Oliver Wendell Holmes's basic attitudes, seeking assurance that this was a man who was "absolutely sane and sound on the great national policies for which we stand in public life." [8] He was explicitly stating the implicit policy most Presidents follow.

Occasionally a President may make an appointment contrary to his own attitudes to balance a situation or to mollify some group not represented on the Court; thus the Kennedy administration was considering seriously the appointment of a conservative Southerner to the Court in order to legitimize the desegregation decisions. Such an action, however, is clearly not in the usual pattern and is probably considered only when a secure majority for the President's position is to be found on the Court. In view of the vagaries of life and the usual rather precarious balance of any majority on the Court, Presidents have usually considered such chivalry a luxury.

Although Presidents have usually been pretty well able to ascertain the views of their appointees in advance, they have sometimes been disappointed. Theodore Roosevelt was classically outraged at Oliver Wendell Holmes's decision in the Northern Securities Case, insisting that he could "carve a judge with more backbone out of a banana." But despite Roosevelt's characteristic towering rages Holmes did represent very faithfully the major outlines of Theodore Roosevelt's ideas on nationalism, strong central government, and Presidential authority, as well as his progressive and humanitarian outlook on social legislation and civil liberties.

Things have not always worked out so well. Wilson's appointee McReynolds not only usually canceled out the vote of Louis Brandeis, but his uncouth surliness also helped drive the third and last Wilson appointee, John Hessin Clarke, off the bench. The Court presided over by Chief Justice Stone from 1941 to 1946—a Court composed almost exclusively of Roosevelt appointees—was profoundly divided by bitterness and inability to agree on principle. Stone himself had been appointed by Coolidge and was fully expected to line up with the conservative wing of the Court, but to the disappointment of Chief Justice Taft he moved increasingly to agreement with the liberals, Holmes and Brandeis.

[8] Lodge to Roosevelt, July 10, 1902, in Lodge, *op. cit.,* **I,** pp. 517–19.

It has been shrewdly noted that one can often tell more about the President from his Supreme Court appointments than by any other single index. Particularly revealing in this respect was the record of Harry Truman's appointees. They tended to be reasonably liberal in their economic decisions but quite conservative in their civil rights and national security rulings. As his subsequent writings and statements to the press showed, this came closer to the core of Harry Truman's personal beliefs than had his activities as President.

Perhaps no other qualification for the Supreme Court bench is so important as political involvement. Schmidhauser tells us that "every member of the Supreme Court except George Shiras held a political post at some time prior to his appointment to the high bench." [9] Even excluding the men whose political connections were minor or judicial like Cardozo—which Schmidhauser somewhat misleadingly does not—most of the justices have had very strong political commitments and, as he suggests, the majority have had predominantly political careers. In various epochs he finds that the proportion of "politicals" on the Court has varied from about 30 per cent in 1920–1932 to 85 per cent in the 1789–1828 period. Substantial numbers of state court judges were appointed to the Supreme Court in the period 1862–1932, and corporate attorneys have constituted about 15–20 per cent of the appointees since 1862. A small number of appointments have been directly from the law schools, and these—Frankfurter, Douglas, and Rutledge—were part of President Roosevelt's effort to expand the field of recruitment for justices; of these only Frankfurter went directly from the lecture hall to the Court.

Secondary to general ideology is the factor of geography. This was particularly true in the early years when each justice rode circuit and was expected to handle cases in his home area. Except for the Chief Justice, geographical considerations were followed until the end of the nineteenth century. No associate justice was named from a state with existing representation on the bench until Stanley Matthews from Ohio was confirmed in 1881. Jefferson was so concerned with geography that he selected Thomas Todd of Kentucky on the designation of the representatives from the newly created "Western" circuit. But as circuit responsibilities declined and then were virtually eliminated, geographical considerations became less significant. After the Civil War even the North-South balance on the Court became unimportant. At the end of Truman's term, for example, the nine sitting

---

[9] Schmidhauser, *op. cit.,* pp. 45–46.

justices came from only five of the ten circuits. Greater diversity of state origins increases the President's freedom of choice, since no permanent rights to a position on the Court can come to be considered as vested in any one state. Massachusetts preserved a virtual strangle hold on the position filled originally by William Cushing; until the appointment of Arthur Goldberg of Illinois in 1962, men from Massachusetts had occupied the position for 140 years. Yet no President today could recognize a claim to the seat on a purely state-of-residence basis.

Since today's geographical consideration is one of general area or region of origin rather than state, the President is relatively free to define these for himself. There is no general agreement on regional distribution in American politics, and the current circuits are geographically artificial anyway. Nor are the general responsibilities of the individual justices in hearing petitions, granting temporary stays, and the like, of sufficient significance to arouse local response or even to require local support. In general, this fact contributes enough flexibility to make geography secondary in importance. When Senator Hill twice successfully objected to President Cleveland's efforts to replace Justice Blatchford with another New Yorker, Cleveland responded by naming Edward White of Louisiana, a state with no representative on the Court. Except for very brief periods, however, there has always been a New Yorker on the bench, a total of 12 justices in all. In terms of years of service, New York has only fractionally less than an average of one justice for every year of the Court's existence.

The geographical considerations that have prevailed have been defined by the President for his political purposes and are increasingly his prerogative. Taft's residence was listed as Connecticut, for example, to overcome objections to the naming of a third Ohioan. Douglas, who insisted upon his Yakima, Washington, residence for political purposes was designated from Connecticut to placate Western Senators who wanted assurances that he would not be considered as having been drawn from their quota of appointments.

B. Judges: Turnover, Vacancies, and Numbers

Unlike other agencies of American government, the Supreme Court is timeless. Congress, the Presidency, most major administrative appointments are characteristically oriented toward the automatic end of their terms of office. American government, a British commentator has observed, is "governed by the calendar and American life appears to regulate itself by the constitutional clock. . . ." [10]

In contrast, the Supreme Court looms as a "continuous constitutional convention" engaged, as Whitehead has put it, in the highly aesthetic task of reconciling an eighteenth-century framework to a twentieth-century society. Life tenure not only gives a feeling of independence to the individual judge; it affects the basic stance of the institution itself.

"Service during good behavior" means that retirement is a product of an act of God or an act of will. In contemporary political terms this means death, resignation, or retirement. Potentially and constitutionally, this might also mean removal by impeachment, but in actuality no justice has ever been removed from office. Impeachment charges were brought against Justice Samuel Chase in the Jeffersonian period; however, the effort succeeded only in demonstrating that, as Jefferson put it, "Impeachment is but a broken reed." There have been four instances of removal of lower court judges, but with one exception—for secessionist views in 1862—upon grounds of bribery and incapacity. Even at the inferior court level as many formal efforts at impeachment have failed as have been successful. Removal because of unpopular decisions has been frowned upon in American politics. At the height of the turn-of-the-century criticism of the Court Theodore Roosevelt ventured to espouse recall of judicial decisions—not of judges themselves—but even here he was careful to make the proposal apply only to state courts, not to the Supreme Court of the United States. Thus the call for the impeachment of Chief Justice Warren by the John Birch Society, which seems to have more of the quality of the Sorelian "myth of the general strike" than of a genuine political program, is a relatively unprecedented form of populistic pressure upon the Court.

Death, on the other hand, is naturally not a stranger to the Court; it has been responsible for over half of the vacancies on the Court. In the early years resignations tended to occur for all sorts of reasons; Chief Justice Jay resigned to assume the governorship of New York, for example. But as the Court's prestige increased, justices found fewer reasons to step down from the bench. In this century John Hessin Clarke resigned to head the League of Nations movement, and Owen J. Roberts resigned a few years later to become

---

[10] Harold Stannard, *The Two Constitutions* (Princeton, D. Van Nostrand, 1949), p. 20.

Dean of the Pennsylvania Law School. In both instances personal relations and declining effectiveness on the Court seem to have been a motivating factor. Most of the other retirements or resignations have been for reasons of ill health or compelling disability.

In general, justices have not voluntarily sought their own retirement and withdrawal from active life. There are indications of a stepped-up rate of retirement since the improvement brought about by the Retirement Act of 1937, particularly since that law makes it possible for a Supreme Court justice to remain active at lower court levels after withdrawing from the rigors of full participation in the Supreme Court. Only in the periods from 1789 to 1796 and from 1937 to the present have the number of resignations and retirements exceeded the number of deaths of Supreme Court members.

Robert Dahl's calculation that each President has had a new appointment to make on the average of every 22 months has generally been accepted as accurate.[11] However, Dahl's estimate includes replacement rates from the early period of Court history when the number of justices was altered by Congress for various purposes and was, for all practical purposes, at or below the current nine. From 1870 through 1963, a period in which the Court has consistently had nine members, the Court had 56 replacements. The average interval since 1937 has been 17 months, reflecting in part the large number of appointments made during the period 1937–41. Table 1 suggests the accelerated replacement rate in recent years.

Table 1

	Years in Office	Appointments
Roosevelt	13	8
Truman	7	4
Eisenhower	8	5
Kennedy	3	2

At this frequency Presidents can expect to appoint about three new Supreme Court justices every four-year term. Dahl dramatically notes that Mr. Roosevelt, in contrast, made no new appointments until 1937, a factor which itself created some difficulty with his Su-

[11] Robert Dahl, "Decision Making in a Democracy: The Supreme Court as a National Policy-Maker," **6** *Journal of Public Law* (1958), pp. 279–95.

preme Court. The ratio for Roosevelt's total term of office suggests that the law of averages finally caught up with the Court and also suggests strongly that 17–18 months is a realistic estimate of the frequency of new appointments.

Retirements and resignations are in part a function of the justices' confidence in a President. Since the justice himself often selects the moment of his departure from the Court, he tends to bear in mind the possible successor that an incoming President might appoint in his place. Justice Duval demanded to know who his successor would be before he would agree to resign. President William Howard Taft once looked at his appointees to the Court and indicated that if any of them died during the wrong administration he would disown them. Disapproving of Hoover and his "liberal" tendencies, Chief Justice Taft indicated he would stay on until "the Bolsheviki" were out of office. The rapidity of retirements after 1937 suggests that some of the old guard members of the Court had been withholding their resignations pending the defeat of President Roosevelt as predicted by the *Literary Digest* in 1936. Justice Roberts himself later concluded that some of the bitterness of the Supreme Court fight might have been avoided had Roosevelt been able to appoint some new justices in his first term.

Although justices can delay their retirements, age eventually takes its toll. Whether justices are better or worse at predicting the election and the tenure of Presidents than the Presidents are at choosing justices and guessing how long who will sit on the Court is a question about which we have little evidence. Senility was once a great problem. Today justices can resign outright with generous pensions or be reassigned to temporary lower court duty if active but less strenuous service is sought. Consequently, the pressures to retire brought to bear upon a partly disabled justice who cannot bear a full load can be greater than in the old days when he would have otherwise suffered financially or been excluded from any further useful contribution. The classic story is of the delegation of colleagues who came to octogenarian Justice Field to suggest his retirement. They began by referring to the occasion years before when Field had led such a mission to speak to Justice Grier. Field's senility was intermittent; occasionally he was as sharp and biting as ever, and they caught him in his old form. "Yes," the old man shot back, sensing what was up, "and a dirtier day's work I never did in my life." [12]

[12] Carl B. Swisher, *Stephen J. Field, Craftsman of the Law* (Washington, D.C.: The Brookings Institution, 1930), p. 444.

The delegation retired crestfallen and empty-handed. Today's justices need feel less self-consciousness. On the contrary; it is now the judge who stays on, not carrying his share of the load when attractive alternatives are available, who is held to be clearly at fault. Yet it is still human nature to attempt to remain, and incumbents generally tend to find reasons to avoid resignation or retirement as long as possible.

There is one additional avenue for creating openings on the Court, now regarded as illegitimate though clearly constitutional. The number of positions on the Court is fixed not by the Constitution but by statute. In the first 80 years of our national experience there was a series of increases and a number of both attempted and successful decreases in the number of justices. Since 1870 Congress has maintained the membership at nine. Roosevelt's proposal to add justices equivalent in number to those who did not retire or resign at the age of 70 was denounced as "Court packing," in violation of the spirit though not the letter of the Constitution. The passage of only three quarters of a century rendered what had once been a commonplace political maneuver into suspect un-Americanism.

But the Constitution still allows changes in the membership, and a recent effort sponsored by the American Bar Association to amend the Constitution to permanently fix the number failed; in 1954 the House Judiciary Committee rejected the Butler Amendment, which would have fixed the number of members at nine and would have deprived Congress of its power to alter the appellate jurisdiction of the Court. As it now stands, altering the number of Justices looms as a tainted but still available weapon to hold down a runaway Court. Congress has no discernible intent to use the power but is obviously reluctant to give it up entirely.

C. Influences in Selection

The process of consideration for appointment to the Supreme Court involves only the President, who nominates, and the Senate, which confirms. The President particularly is free to consult as widely or as restrictively as he chooses. Because of his access to information about proposed retirement, his bargaining power over the nominations and the candidates, and the general respect for his office, the President can to a large extent control the timing of retirement and the announcement of new appointments. This in turn gives him great power to restrict or divulge information relative to his intentions concerning any new appointment. The variable of publicity in turn affects to a large extent the access that other people will have to the appointment. Thus the President can make the process as open and as public or as restricted and as private as he desires.

In view of the abundance of candidates, sponsorship by someone with access to the President is normally necessary. The fiction that the justices are not active candidates will often restrict consideration. Tradition has it that Justice Catron was nominated after his wife went to the White House and actively solicited the nomination from the retiring President Jackson. While other candidates have been extremely diligent in their own behalf, they have usually been more circumspect as well. We do know, however, that many justices as well as unsuccessful candidates actively canvassed all the support they could mobilize both in the Senate and the administration.

Of the two major influences, that of the Presidency is clearly the greater. The President chooses from among a large range of candidates and presents one for Senate consideration. Rejection by the Senate is unlikely, and in this century has proven to be almost impossible. There have been eras when the Senate effectively used its power to deny confirmation—mostly for partisan reasons, and in one period for ideological reasons over slavery—but in the twentieth century only John Parker of North Carolina was refused confirmation, and that by one vote, at the height of the controversy over the Supreme Court's conservative social attitudes in the 1920s and 1930s.

The respective roles of President and Senate in judicial appointments present a curious balance of power. All federal judges are chosen in the same way, yet the respective power of these institutions varies with the level of the court involved. The federal district courts, by law and tradition wholly within the borders of a single state, have been under the primary influence of Senate selection. Joseph P. Harris has even spoken of the process at that level as selection by the Senate with veto by the President.[13] In general the principles of senatorial courtesy, while hardly as inflexible as it is often portrayed, means that the President will usually abide by the wishes of senators from his own party.

Senators will not sustain the objections of a fellow senator whom they do not respect and will seek to vindicate a President for whom they have special regard. Nevertheless, Presidents ignore the recom-

---

[13] Joseph P. Harris, *The Advice and Consent of the Senate* (Berkeley: University of California Press, 1953), pp. 314–15.

mendations of senators in these matters at their own risk. A President may defy one senator of his party if he has at least some backing from another in the same state. In 1936 Senator Bilbo of Mississippi, for example, failed to block confirmation of a nomination personally obnoxious to him. Further, it is axiomatic that the President cannot defy both senators from a state, and yet Shiras of Pennsylvania was successfully appointed in this manner.

The senators do not act as free agents in these matters. Rather, they usually suggest the names of individuals who have strong political roots in their home states. In short, federal district judgeships largely reflect the complexion of the organizational forces in the states involved. Although Presidents have fought this tradition and some have been successful in developing their own candidates, the pattern is sufficiently strong to be stated in the form of a rule.

Midway between the district courts and the Supreme Court are the courts of appeals. These embrace several states on a regional basis. With three exceptions, the number of judges on each court of appeals is sufficient to allow each state in the circuit to be represented on the bench. As a consequence, there is a balance between the geographic claims of a state and more general standards applied to the region as a whole. The President thus has more bargaining power, but is still not completely free. There is therefore delicate equilibrium between presidential discretion and senatorial prerogative. Presidents have gauged their powers in various fashions at this level. Franklin Roosevelt, for example, paid virtually no attention to senatorial recommendations for this office; most Presidents have been more deferential.

President Kennedy, who appointed an extraordinary number of district judges (about 10 per cent of all ever appointed) to effect a badly needed expansion, had a bit more freedom than normal as a consequence. He further pressed this advantage by spotting capable candidates and generating local support for them, though not publicly reversing the usual processes of nomination. Since his choices were of unusually superior quality, drawing almost unstinted praise from the American Bar Association as the best group ever nominated by one President, the necessary local endorsements were generally forthcoming.

At the Supreme Court level, however, the President is largely independent of any truly restrictive senatorial direction. His geographic freedom means that no senator can claim an appointment as a matter of right; regional considerations, when they apply, may lead to senatorial pressure but are not a matter of prerogative—which is a vital distinction.

The balance of political forces involved in the selection of a nominee is also significant to the ideological complexion of the Court. The Presidency has clearly been more "liberal" in American politics in this century than the Congress; the Senate has emerged in the last quarter of a century as the more "liberal" of the two houses. Basically, both developments are a reversal of the tradition of most of the nineteenth century, when the House of Representatives was regarded as the populist branch of the government. This reversal has been paralleled by a reversal of the ideological alignment of the Court. The system of pulleys and gears that results in the selection of a Supreme Court justice actually translates subtle trends in the Senate and the Presidency into bolder and more evident differences on the Court. Reflecting its selection by a conservative Presidency and a Senate not even selected by popular vote, the Supreme Court was throughout the greater part of our history a conservative bulwark. The great attacks on the Court by the Jeffersonians and Jacksonians, the Populists and the Progressives, were all attacks of the "Left" upon what they regarded as an instrument of privilege for the upper classes. In the struggle over slavery, too, the Court was on the side of entrenched conservatism, as committed as the Presidency and the Senate, its chief patrons.

In the twentieth century all this has been reversed. The modern Supreme Court reflects a Presidency sensitive to the Electoral College votes of large, liberal states with urban predominance and a Senate increasingly responsive to much the same pattern. Presidential appointments take into account senatorial attitudes but reflect more nearly the President's own and tend to make the Court more liberal than either branch of Congress, and certainly more so than the House of Representatives. As a consequence, opponents of the Court in recent years have for the first time in history complained that the justices are too liberal, and the Court has vied with the Presidency for leadership in innovation.

The federal district judge is more likely to have been the product of a routine political career than a distinguished lawyer, legal scholar, or thinker. (This is not to say that distinguished legal scholars or men of legal ability are *never* recognized by local political organizations.) In consequence, the Supreme Court may find that its decisions are not always happily received by the lower federal courts, which, in most instances, must implement decisions.

There is a significant measure of difference between the state and federal benches in both the manner of selection and the type of person chosen. Of course, the professional orientation that is esteemed at all levels means that judges do hold common attitudes on many issues. Indeed, as we have noticed, many Supreme Court justices have come directly from the highest state court bench or are related to judges in such positions. Nevertheless, there is a real difference in the character of the membership of the two benches which, when reinforced by differences in state interests and sharpened by the slogans of states rights, often leads to sharp disagreement and occasionally even to defiance.

But it is not only the allocation of power between Presidency and Senate that influences selection. The distribution of power within these institutions is also significant. In the Senate the primary power and responsibility for such matters is allocated to the Judiciary Committee; within the executive branch it is the Department of Justice that is pre-eminent.

In the early years of the Republic the agency of the executive branch charged with the routine work in connection with judicial appointments was the office of the Secretary of State. For about a century now, however, the Department of Justice has handled this mission. It prepares files on prospective candidates as well as taking care of the paper work preparatory to the appointment. In this it is aided by the Administrative Office of the U.S. Courts (created in 1939). The task of assembling names and data is, of course, one that involves a good deal of discretion and power.

Again, as the President has relied more heavily upon the Department of Justice for such information, so has the tendency to choose judges from among officials of the Department increased—a good index of the growth of its power and responsibility. The Court of Appeals for the District of Columbia has had numerous appointments from the Department of Justice and other governmental legal offices. In the District, of course, the President's political obligations and accountability to local party operations are nil. The Attorney General and his subordinates are not only in a position to make a claim for themselves but can also help or hinder other candidates. Thus did Attorney General Jackson facilitate the choice of Mr. Justice Frankfurter.

While other Cabinet members may or may not be consulted by the President, the Attorney General will always be consulted. The weight his advice carries, of course, varies from President to President depending on his relationship with the Attorney General, but it would be a mortal insult if he did not at least allow the Attorney General to express his opinion.

It is the responsibility of the Department of Justice not only to examine the merits of candidates but also to suggest the names of possible nominees. In recent years this function has fallen to the Deputy Attorney General—Judge Walsh under President Eisenhower and Messrs. White and Katzenbach under Mr. Kennedy.

Of course, the President may go outside his official family to obtain advice. Newspaperman and author Irving Brant, for example, had a rather surprising influence in Roosevelt's judicial appointments, and it was largely his continued interest over the years in the nomination of Wiley Rutledge that finally secured Rutledge a court of appeals position and eventually a justiceship of the United States Supreme Court. Distinguished judges and attorneys may also be consulted. Justice Brennan apparently owes his nomination largely to the sponsorship of the late Chief Justice Vanderbilt of the New Jersey Supreme Court, a judge, political leader, and scholarly entrepreneur of considerable note. Former justices have also been consulted from time to time.

Although the very first Congress had a Senate Judiciary Committee, it was, like all other committees at that time, *ad hoc*.[14] When, in the first half of the nineteenth century, a system of permanent committees was established, the Judiciary Committee was one of these. Use of the Committee for review of appointments was at first sporadic and intermittent but had become regular practice by 1868. Prior to that, reference of nominations to the Committee was generally reserved for controversial appointments. The Judiciary Committee has thus been a battleground for nominations and has been instrumental in the success or defeat of candidates for two centuries, but principally in the last one.

In the early years the Committee was not by any means the sole or even the controlling factor in the outcome. Thus, Matthews and Lamar were confirmed over its objections. But as the traditions of the Senate have become more institutionalized, so has been the deference to Committee determinations.

All 300 or so members of the Judiciary Committee since its inception have been lawyers. Many of these have aspired to the Supreme

[14] On the work of the Judiciary Committee see David Farrelly, "Operational Aspects of the Senate Judiciary Committee," Ph.D. Dissertation, Princeton University, 1949 (University Microfilms).

Court. Six have reached the Court; two others were refused confirmation, and two declined. On the whole the Committee has been a desirable training ground and stepping stone for those with judicial ambitions. The last two former members appointed, however, were not members of the Committee at the time, and its significance as a stepping stone currently appears to be in eclipse.

The true importance of the Senate's power of a confirmation has in this century not been found in its formal power of rejection but in the contact afforded in the preliminary stages to the senators with the Department of Justice and the President. In this century the Senate has rejected only one nominee, but its scrutiny of nominations has become more intensive. The failure to discover and explore the Ku Klux Klan background of Mr. Justice Black—a background which all admit does not seem to have influenced his decisions—resulted in decisions by the Senate and the Judiciary Committee to hold preliminary hearings over subsequent nominations. Although in form the ban on questions concerning particular matters that will come before the Court in the immediate future has been preserved, the questioning in fact is designed to scrutinize a nominee's probable attitudes toward current constitutional issues. At the height of the criticism of the Court by segregationists and those who felt that the national security decisions of recent years were unfortunate, prospective justices were even asked to affirm that the court had no right to change the Constitution and to pledge themselves to be more responsive to the intent of Congress. This absurd and naïve oath was sought not in the name of the Senate or indeed of the whole Committee but rather by an individual senator. Perhaps the most extreme form of ideological questioning occurred when Justice Brennan was asked to indicate that he would follow "not papal decrees and doctrines but the laws and precedents of this nation." Over the misgivings of Senator Kefauver as to the appropriateness of this type of questioning, Mr. Brennan assured the senators that he took the oath of office "just as unreservedly as I know you did and every member and everyone else of our faith in whatever office, elective or appointive, he may hold." [15]

Although the questioning goes on, the virtually unbroken recent tradition of the Senate to accept nominees as they are presented by the President also continues. One might assume from the absence of

[15] "Nomination of William Joseph Brennan, Jr." U.S. Judiciary Committee, 85th Congress, 1st Session, 1957, p. 33.

rejections that there has been a decline in the influence of the Senate. Actually, it is much more complex than that: a major reason for the absence of rejections is the better and more careful consultation of the Senate as a whole and the Committee in particular prior to the submission of names. So, for example, in order to clear the road for the nomination of Justice Douglas, President Roosevelt and his Department of Justice in effect promised two lower court appointments to Western states.[16] In the case of the nomination of Senator Black, however, President Roosevelt acted decisively and independently, precisely to secure a nomination that would be unpalatable but incontestable.

This greater involvement of the Senate Judiciary Committee in the prenomination stage goes a long way toward explaining the dramatic reduction of refusals to confirm in this century. Prior to that time, the Senate had rejected over one-quarter of the names presented to it; since 1898, the rejections constitute only one out of the more than forty names presented to the Senate. The rate of rejection is less than one-tenth that of the 18th and 19th centuries. While a good deal of the higher rate in the early periods reflects party differences in the control of the Presidency in the Senate, the increased communication and cooperation of the Senate into the nomination process plays a major role.

In the informal early stages individual senators can be crucial determinants of the outcome. Senator Lodge's espousal of Holmes's candidacy over a period of years was eventually successful. Many a justice has owed his position to his friendship with or sponsorship by a senator. Indeed, some of the more distinguished members of the Court—Samuel Miller comes readily to mind—had very little visible qualification except such a relationship.

In recent years a new force has entered the picture, the American Bar Association, which has long sought better and less political appointments to the judiciary. Their emphasis has been on the lower courts, where indeed the qualifications are more nearly matters of purely legal competence than on the Supreme Court itself.

The Committee on the Federal Judiciary of the Bar Association was established in 1945. Cooperation with the Senate Judiciary Committee began early, but Bar Association activity was limited to statements of approval or disapproval at Committee hearings. Informal clearance began in the very last weeks of the Truman administration.

[16] Burke, *op. cit.,* pp. 152–53.

Attorney General Brownell and his Deputy Attorney General continued to work with the Bar Association Committee but exacted an agreement that the Committee would confine itself to rating suggestions made by others rather than trying to advance its own nominees. This was accepted by the Bar Association and has remained the practice.

President Eisenhower's position was that no name would be submitted for district or appellate judgeships if the Bar Association's judgment was unfavorable. But efforts by the Committee to influence and evaluate the nominations of Chief Justice Warren and Mr. Justice Harlan were rejected by the Department of Justice on the grounds that Supreme Court appointments were the President's own prerogative and could be shared with no one. Unexpectedly, however, President Eisenhower asked that Mr. Justice Brennan be evaluated by the American Bar Association, and subsequently the Committee was consulted in other Supreme Court appointments as well.[17]

The Committee has established that no lawyer over 60 years old should be confirmed unless rated as "well qualified or exceptionally well qualified" and that in no event will an endorsement be given to a lawyer past the age of 64. The Eisenhower administration held to the practice of giving only one name for each judgeship, and the Bar Association then indicated its approval or disapproval. Attorney General Kennedy's Department gave up to six names for each vacancy, assuring the executive greater freedom in its final choice. The Kennedy administration refused to accept unconditionally the prior practice of giving the Committee a veto. A major criterion by the Association has been the question of age, and the Kennedy Department of Justice took the position that it was a better judge than the Bar Association of whether other qualities overweighed the possible imminent retirement of the nominee. Inasmuch as the Bar Association itself has not been free of ideological commitments—it has long been known as a conservative organization, and its leaders opposed the nomination of Mr. Justice Brandeis—the reluctance to grant them a veto power is understandable. Yet some respected observers, including *The New York Times,* believe that President Eisenhower's iron-clad rule was best. In any event, Presidents are always unhappy at

[17] See Edward Fox, Jr., "The Work of the American Bar Association Federal Judiciary Committee," in Schmidhauser, ed., *Constitutional Law in the Political Process* (Chicago: Rand McNally, 1963), pp. 182–93, and D. D. Eisenhower, *Mandate for Change* (Garden City: Doubleday, 1963), pp. 226–27.

opposing the Association, and it is embarrassing to have to defend a nominee who is not rated as professionally qualified for judgeship.

The inclusion of the Bar Association in the process has drawn considerable attention, but it must not be overlooked that this has come about because the other participants have felt they will gain thereby. The Judiciary Committee, when it worked alone, had indifferent success in gaining prenomination clearance. The entry of the Bar Association has strengthened the hand of the Judiciary Committee, for the two committees work closely together. The President can use the professional ratings as an instrument for refusing unworthy local suggestions for district courts and thus gains leverage in dealing with party organizations.

The growing importance of the Department of Justice attorneys and other government solicitors is even more striking in the lower courts than at the Supreme Court level, particularly in the courts of the District of Columbia where there is no intervening local political organization to present strong candidates of its own. Similarly, potential judges who have been blocked by their local organizations or by senatorial courtesy but who have strong backing at the presidential level have often found a place of refuge on the District of Columbia courts. The staffing of the District's courts by government attorneys is of definite significance, particularly in the area of administrative law, for the Court of Appeals of the District of Columbia has special responsibilities for many appeals from administrative agencies. Whether this pattern will be seriously altered by the conferral of voting privilege for the Presidency upon the residents of the District remains to be seen.

The American Bar Association has been openly critical of the appointment of large numbers of government lawyers to the courts. It has even suggested in its official resolutions the impropriety of the Department of Justice, itself the principal litigant before the courts, in having any part in the selection of judges. In 1958 it set up a committee to explore and promote a process of selection by a commission, which would have eliminated the participation of the Department of Justice. Only four years later, however, apparently satisfied by the success of its program in influencing judicial selections through the Committee on Judicial Selection, the Association discontinued the special committee on nonpartisan selection of the federal judiciary and has not renewed its criticism of the Department's role in selection. The comments of Mr. Harold Gallegher and the report of the committee suggest that left-handed efforts to minimize the role of the Department of Justice did not enhance the Association's right-handed drive for greater cooperation with the Department in the selection process.[18]

D. The Road to the Court

How then do aspiring judges come to the attention of those who are in a position to choose them? What is the route they travel through life to arrive at the ultima Thule of the Supreme Court? It is obvious from our previous discussion that part of the secret lies in being born of the proper parents and thus obtaining the proper background and ambition, though which is causative and which derivative is problematical. Going to the proper schools, both undergraduate and graduate, is also valuable. Lifetime friendships with future Presidents or senators or attorneys general are invaluable and somewhat unpredictable assets which have helped many a potential judge obtain his post. And, of course, he must decide to become a lawyer.

The legal profession provides several branches which can lead to a judicial career. Principally, these are the practice of law, legal education, or a career of public service. The practice of private law usually and almost invariably must be accompanied by political activity in order to lead to the Court. Law school professorships were stepping stones only during the Roosevelt New Deal period.

Public service is, in short, the principal route. The main possibilities of this kind are the lower judiciary, elective political office, and executive and administrative positions.

Two strong trends may be noted in the pattern of the past. First, those involved in or close to the actual organized system for judicial selection obviously and significantly increase their chances for accession to the Court. Second, at least in this century, there is a distinct difference in the type of justice selected by the two political parties. The standard Republican choices have had professional and judicial careers on a local level. The standard Democratic choices have been much more obviously politically and nationally oriented. Both of these sweeping generalizations require more extensive discussion and more exacting qualification.

The advantages of being President emerge clearly from the figures in both absolute and relative terms. Only one President has himself been appointed to the Court. Yet even this figure is rather substantial

---

[18] *Reports of the American Bar Association, 1962*, pp. 141–42 and 744–45.

considering the base of 35 potential nominees (actually 27 if one excludes those who died in office). In addition, the single presidential example may well be an indication of the desires of many of the others. Most Presidents have felt that further officeholding would not be consistent with their dignity; even William Howard Taft felt that the chief justiceship alone represented no loss of face. Though the Taft appointment was *sui generis,* what is revealing about the incident is the extent to which a President could, if he wished—together with good fortune—set the stage for his own choice by a future President. Indications are that Taft, as President, passed over Hughes, a younger man, and elevated White, a Democrat of advanced age, with the understanding that the latter would vacate the chief justiceship when a Republican President took office so that Taft himself might be appointed to the position. How explicit this agreement was is not known; Taft felt he could only suffer philosophically when, in the first months of the Harding administration, no resignation came from White. Finally, in May 1921, White died, still in office, and Harding saw fit to confer the vacancy upon Taft.[19]

The power of the President is as clearly revealed in the choice of Cabinet members as justices. Not only is there a predominance of selection from the key Cabinet positions, but rivaling all others in frequency of appointment to the Court is the position of Attorney General.

Four eras can be roughly delineated with regard to choices from the Department of Justice. In the early years the practice was neither institutionalized nor respected; such appointments were limited to Levi Lincoln, who declined, and Taney, who had held an intervening office. The three decades from 1840 saw many chosen but few called, as party and institutional jealousy resulted in Senate refusal to confirm the President's men. After the Department began to assume responsibility in the selection process there seems to have been a lull even in the nomination of its own men to the bench. However, there has been regular and frequent appointment from the Department since the nomination of McKenna in 1898. Seven of the nine Attorneys General who served in the Court (and of the 15 ever nominated by a President) were chosen in those 66 years. Ten of the 39 justices appointed in that same interval had seen service in the Department.

[19] C. Herman Pritchett, *The Roosevelt Court* (New York: Macmillan, 1948), pp. 17–18.

Similarly, former senators have often served on the Court. Indeed, at first sight the total number of ex-senators among the justices might suggest even the advantage of the Senate over the Presidency as a recruiting ground; some commentators have indeed accepted such a conclusion. But the fallacy lies in considering rates solely in terms of those who have achieved the position, taking the absolute number of individuals having a characteristic as indicating the advantage of that attribute. If one reasons, not backward from the attributes of those who have held the office, but in career line forward, from previous position to the outcome, a different perspective emerges.

This criticism of the method of taking characteristics of incumbents incidentally is of quite general application not in any sense limited to the Court. It would be appropriate to reconsider a number of characterizations of what constitutes "availability," and what are the stepping stones to higher position in the light of probability of the stepping stone proving the means to a desired end. Table 2 below illustrates the different perspective that emerges when potential base and achievement both are considered rather than the latter alone.

When one takes into account the total number of senators who might have been eligible to hold the office, and indeed might have been close personal associates of the President, as against the total number of persons who have held individual Cabinet positions, the *relative* advantage of, let us say, the Attorney General's position over a mere senatorship quickly emerges (see Table 2). There have been about 1,600 senators through history, compared to some 60 Attorneys General. The surprisingly strong showing of members of the House of Representatives in the total number of Supreme Court justices also becomes less impressive when one considers the relatively greater base number from which it is drawn. Finally, the assumption that the state supreme court is the best possible stepping stone loses its validity when one considers the unknown but obviously high number of potential holders of that office in 50 states with benches typically composed of seven to nine members and characterized by a fairly rapid turnover.

The importance of the Cabinet is underscored by the fact that even if one eliminates the Attorney General's position the number of justices drawn from the Cabinet equals the number drawn from the Senate, though the total number of such officeholders is only one quarter that of the senators. On the other hand, access to the President does not always insure popularity in the Senate, as the one-third rejection rate for Cabinet members indicates.

Table 2 Governmental Offices as Steppingstones to Supreme Court Positions 1789–1964

Office	Justices with This Experience	Nominees (Rejected or Declined) Holding This Office	All with This Experience (Approx.)	% Nominated for the Court	% Who Served as Justices
President	1	(0-0)	27 *	3.7 *	3.7 *
Senate	14	(3-3)	1,600	1.25 *	.88 *
House of Representatives	18	(4-2)	9,100	.26 *	.19 *
Senate Judiciary Committee	6	(2-2)	300	3.3	2.0
Cabinet (all positions)	22	(7-2)	465	6.6 *	4.7 *
Attorney General	9	(4-2)	66	22.7	13.6
Secretary of State	3	(1-0)	53	7.5 *	5.66 *
Solicitor General	3	(0-0)	32	9.4	9.4
Court of Appeals	15	(1-0)	275	5.8	5.45
State Courts	35	(5-0)	not ascertained		
Governors	8	(2-0)	"	"	
State Legislators	23	(4-0)	"	"	
Federal District Court	9	(0-0)	1,225	.73	.73

* Presidents' total based upon those completing the term of office on the assumption that no Supreme Court appointment would occur prior to that time. This total and others should be discounted by an undetermined factor, since not all were attorneys.

Derived from *Biographical Directory of the American Congress 1774–1961; Legislative History of the U. S. Court of Appeals; Federal Cases;* Typewritten list of district judges, 1896–1937, Library of Congress Law Reference Division; listing of judges 1937 to present through courtesy of Administrative Office United States Courts; *White's Conspectus; World Almanac.*

The significance of House service dwindles when one takes as a measure not simply those justices who have served in it but only those who were appointed directly from it. Only Wayne was a member of the House when nominated, and although Baldwin held no other office after serving in the House, he had practiced law for eight years prior to joining the Court. All of the other 16 with House experience had held other, higher (in terms of their value as steppingstones to the Court) positions in intervening years.

Fifteen justices saw previous service on a court of appeals, the next lower rung in the federal judiciary.[20] Two of these—Taft and Vinson—held major national administrative posts in intervening years

[20] "Legislative History of the United States Circuit Courts of Appeals and the Judges Who Served, 1801–1958," U. S. House Committee on the Judiciary, 86th Congress, 2d Session.

before going to the Court. Of the remainder, seven had served for four years or less before elevation to the Supreme Court, Whittaker having served only nine months. It cannot be said that these figures indicate a regular promotion system. The majority of such nominations to the Court are made by the very administration, or the immediately succeeding administration of the same party, that made the lower court appointment.

There is a pronounced partisan difference in the number of elevations from the courts of appeals that is part of the broader and more far-reaching pattern of differences already noted. Twelve out of the 15, including five of the six with above average length of service on a court of appeals, made their way to the Supreme Court through the good graces of Republican Presidents. Three of these were nominal Democrats; inasmuch as they were from border and Southern states it would appear that Republican Presidents have had more freedom of choice in making appointments from that region. Sherman Minton was the justice with the longest court of appeals service to be elevated by a Democratic President, his old Senate friend Harry Truman, after eight and a half years on the Seventh Circuit Court.

Three justices have been confirmed for all levels—district court, court of appeals, and Supreme Court—though only Blatchford and Whittaker have actually so served, insomuch as Day resigned before assuming the district judgeship. Judges of the courts of appeals or district courts are either promoted soon or not at all; a new administration tends to have rather different sources of information and evaluation and is unlikely to view the candidates the same way.

Appointment directly from the district courts is quite rare. Only six justices were sitting on district courts at the time of their selection. Three of these were appointed during 1826–41, a period in which the court of appeals was in limbo. The most recent such choice was that of Sanford in 1923. In spite of Peltason's conclusion that promotion from circuit judge to the Supreme Court is unusual, it seems fair to conclude that the federal judiciary remains a primary source of recruitment for the Supreme Court.[21] In terms of both absolute numbers and relative possibilities—even allowing for the fact that many legislators are not lawyers—federal judgeships must be rated as equal to, or better than, a senatorship as a possible stepping stone to the Court. The fact, however, that only two of the promoted judges served on the Court of Appeals for as long as a decade indi-

[21] Jack Peltason, *Federal Courts in the Political Process* (New York: Random House, 1955), p. 32.

cates that those positions ratify or symbolize "justiciability" rather than create or add to it. Appointment to the appeals court suggests availability; it is not the record achieved there that contributes to or causes future appointments. Sitting judges like Clarke, Lurton, and Minton, as well as former judges like Vinson and Day, have been elevated. Strikingly common has been the pattern of presidential favor for a quite recent appointee of his own; the same factors that influenced the President in first naming a lower court judge often operate and are sufficient for choice at the Supreme Court level itself. The Eisenhower administration, in particular, committed to a principle of previous judicial experience for Supreme Court justices, used this "bootstrap" method of appointment. President Eisenhower elevated no less than three judges from the lower federal judiciary, but every one had been originally appointed during his own administration.

The potentialities of state office are not as easy to evaluate. The number of justices who have had such experience is considerable; two members of the present Court were elevated directly from state office. But the total number of candidates with such experience is dispersed in 50 state histories and is less readily available. In the absence of fair figures it nonetheless seems safe to say that, proportionate to the number of officeholders, justices appointed to the Court have probably always been more often drawn from federal sources than from state. It is also apparent that the stepping-stone offices have grown in number more rapidly on the federal than on the state level. Such federal positions have grown fourfold, although the average length of officeholding has also probably generally increased. While the Cabinet has experienced a somewhat smaller increase than, for example, the Senate, this is more than compensated for by the growth of the Department of Justice, adding the Solicitor General and assistant attorneys general to the list of eligibles, as well as prominent semijudicial regulatory posts in the Commissions.

But changes have taken place above and beyond these numerical facts. Ulmer has studied Court appointments over certain time periods and concludes that there has been continuous erosion of the significance of state experience as a qualification. Further, there seems to have been a loss of emphasis on both levels on judicial and legislative experience and a gain in the importance of administrative experience.[22]

[22] S. S. Ulmer, "Public Office in the Social Background of Supreme Court Justices," 21 *American Journal of Economics and Sociology,* pp. 56–68, esp. pp. 64–65.

Table 3 Party Difference Profile, Previous Experience of Supreme Court Appointees, 1900–1964 (by percentage)

I. Previous governmental service, justices appointed by Democratic and Republican Presidents.

Party of Appointing President	U. S. Senate and House	Cabinet and Federal Administration	Federal, State and Local Courts	Federal and State Lawyers	Governor and Other State Office	President	No Public Office	N
Repub.	15.0	20.0	65.0	55.0	10	5	0	20
Democ.	29.4	52.9	29.4	64.7	5.9	0	11.7	17

II. Last public office prior to appointment, justices appointed by Democratic and Republican Presidents.

Party of Appointing President	U. S. Senate and House	Cabinet and Federal Administration	Federal, State and Local Courts	Federal and State Lawyers	Governor and Other State Office	President	No Public Office	N
Repub.	0	10	60	15	10	5	0	20
Democ.	17.6	47.0	17.6	5.9	0	0	11.7	17

Source: Derived from unpublished data supplied by Joseph Schlesinger; revised and updated through appointment of Mr. Justice Goldberg.

These shifts follow logically from the spectacular growth of the number of administrative positions at both levels and from presidential emancipation from geographic considerations and, therefore, from Senate suggestions which tend to be local in concern. Left largely on his own in picking a respectable candidate, the President tends to choose from within his political family.

While this tendency affects both parties, there are definite differences between the two parties, the Democrats being particularly inclined to select at the federal level and within the administrative category, including Cabinet members, the Republicans leaning more toward state court, gubernatorial, and federal court promotions. Only two Republican members of the Court in this century have been Attorneys General, to four on the Democratic side. No Democratic President, up to the swearing in of President Lyndon Johnson in 1963, failed to elevate at least one governmental attorney, while Eisenhower made five appointments in eight years without a single appointment from the national political area—unless one considers as such the appointment of Governor Warren of California. Similarly, of the five senators appointed in this century, four were Democratic appointments. Only Sutherland—not then serving in office— was a Republican. All three appointments made directly from the Senate were Democratic appointments.

In contrast, two out of three gubernatorial appointments, seven out of 10 elevations of court of appeals judges, and all justices who were elevated from high state courts were Republican appointments. The one Democrat among the state court judges who reached the Supreme Court—Brennan—was appointed by President Eisenhower. At least one commentator has suggested that the figures demonstrate that the Republican Presidents have been more conscientious in their application of professional and legal standards.[23] Yet considering the far greater reputations for effectiveness of the Democratic appointees in this century, especially on the Supreme Court level but on the lower court levels as well, one is tempted to suggest that the Democrats may in fact have had a keener perception of the proper balance of legal ability and political instinct in their choices for the judiciary. It may well be that Democratic Presidents have understood and acted upon a keener estimate of the real nature of the Court itself.

At the same time it would appear that part of the trouble with a "liberal" Court may be the decline of easy communication between

[23] Burke, *op. cit.,* pp. 164–83, 243–46.

the state courts and the Supreme Court. The action of the Conference of State Chief Justices in attacking the Court in August of 1958 and thereby allying itself with critics of recent Court doctrine reflects the pull of different political forces upon the two court systems. But it also may be related to awareness of the state judges of their progressively smaller chances of appointment to the Supreme Court. It is only a trifle fanciful to suggest that behind this antagonism there may be an institutional status loss comparable to the personal status anxiety that often motivates radical political behavior. The Republican party is, of course, more attuned to the wave lengths of prevailing opinion on the state courts. But, as Eisenhower proved, there is also Democratic talent of Supreme Court caliber on the state courts.

Conclusions

The study of recruitment for the Court should ultimately yield answers to two related questions. Evidence on the background characteristics of the justices casts some light on the sharing of power and responsibility of various groupings in our society and raises some questions as to whether this is a proper, desirable, and effective distribution. This is the representational question. There is also the question of the relation between a justice's background and his effectiveness on the Court. This can be dubbed the functional problem.

The Court has been on the whole about as representative in terms of nationality and religion as the Presidency and Congress, less so as to race and sex. All of our major political institutions, however, would raise eyebrows of an efficient fair employment commission.

The American public accepts the monopoly of lawyers and also expects a substantial number of justices to be appointed from prominent positions of public service. It seems obvious that the background and middle-class social characteristics this implies has had a pronounced effect on American constitutional law. Yet in recent years justices with this background have profoundly altered—though less than headlines might suggest—the basic principles of constitutional law.

The new trend toward selection of justices with federal and administrative experience has been paralleled by a shift in constitutional law toward the sanctioning of national power. But it has not been shown that one is either the cause or effect of the other. There are many theories about the connection between a man's career background and his voting behavior on the Court, but no proof.

It seems unlikely that the gross methods currently used in the social sciences will give us reliable results when applied to the small number of test cases available in the persons of Supreme Court justices. Further, the backgrounds of these men, regardless of their voting behavior, exhibit striking similarities as well as differences. Also, prior to their appointments these men are scrutinized in terms other than the gross ones applicable to the study of mass data—i.e., in terms of their public stands on known issues. Yet Nagel used one of the crudest of categories—party affiliation—to study state judges and found pronounced differences in their attitudes on divorce, the Democrats, incidentally, being the more lenient.[24] More fruitful findings on the Supreme Court level are undoubtedly possible.

As the number of appointments from state courts has declined, the cry for more justices with such experience has gone up. Although even President Eisenhower accepted the importance of previous judicial experience, the record seems to suggest strongly the absence of such a necessity. Former Justice Frankfurter has argued that the business of the Supreme Court is so unique a combination of law and politics that previous experience either on state courts or on lower federal courts, though hardly disqualifying, is not particularly advantageous. Rather, the justice's qualities of mind and distinct perception of necessity should be scrutinized and evaluated. Many of the great justices, like Marshall, Miller, Stone, Brandeis, and Hughes, had no previous judicial record; others, like Holmes and Cardozo, did. "One is entitled to say without qualification," Frankfurter has said, "that the correlation between previous judicial experience and judicial greatness is zero." [25]

[24] Stuart Nagel, "Political Party Affiliation and Judges' Decisions," **55** *American Political Science Review* (1961), pp. 843–50.

[25] Felix Frankfurter, "The Supreme Court Mirror of Justices," **23** *Vital Speeches,* May 1, 1957, p. 436.

CHAPTER 2

Recruitment: Cases, Parties, and Lawyers

A. Courts and Litigation: Some Generalizations

SOCIAL LIFE is characterized by a welter of transactions, the vast bulk of which are regulated by internalized and habitual behavior, having no overt relationship to the standards of law. The parent generally pays the costs when his child heaves a brick through a window, though in most instances he has no legal liability. Stewart Macaulay has shown that even in a cutthroat competitive industry like paper-container production, few truly enforceable contracts are ever negotiated.[1] More reliance is placed upon the need for a good business reputation or on personal relationships and trust than upon resort to legal action. Durkheim's suggestion that trust in everyday transactions must precede legal enforcement seems to be truer to the evidence of anthropology than Hobbes's notion that murderously unpredictable paranoids could create a society through the threat of force alone.

Resort to the courts is the exception and clearly not the rule. When disputes arise, people usually try to settle them outside the legal system. "The trouble situations of society," as Llewellyn called them, are first referred to a whole congeries of semiprivate agencies—the marriage counselor, the minister, the family leader. Even the creation of formal institutions for arbitration—a private legal system—is more likely than recourse to the public courts. Even when litigation is initiated, it is more often the opening wedge in a process of bargaining than the prelude to decision by judges. Even cases that have gone through the first stages of the legal process are more likely than not to be settled through eventual private agreement. It is not too much to say that the legal order exists more to force agreement to be made privately outside of the legal system than to arrange such agreements itself. At least that is the evidence suggested by a study of personal

---

[1] Stewart Macaulay, "Non-Contractual Relations in Business: A Preliminary Study," **28** *American Sociological Review* (1963), pp. 55–67; Julius Cohen, *et al., Parental Authority* (New Brunswick: Rutgers University Press, 1958).

liability cases filed in New York City made by the Columbia University Project for Effective Justice.[2] The Project found that approximately 193,000 accident victims sought recovery for damages, with 154,000 of these retaining an attorney. Only about 77,000 cases are, however, sued. By the time of trial this dwindles to 7,000, with only 2,500 actually reaching the verdict stage. The rate of attrition is obviously steep; even among the cases that reach trial nearly two thirds are settled out of court! Only about 1 per cent of the entire number were in fact adjudicated.

Table 4

Stage	Number of Cases	Per Cent of Total
Recovery sought	193,000	100
Attorney retained	154,000	80
Suit instituted	77,000	40
Readiness for trial signified	48,000	25
Trial commenced	7,000	3
Verdict reached	2,500	1

Source: Adapted from Franklin, *et al.,* "Accidents, Money and the Law," **61** *Columbia Law Review* (1961), pp. 10–13.

To be sure, personal liability suits are notoriously a pretext for bargaining, but the general picture of formal decision as the last resort for the resolution of civil disagreements rather than the normal course of procedure seems to comport with what we know of social life.

An early study by Clark and Shulman found that even of cases filed only 17 per cent of contract cases, 16 per cent of automobile negligence cases, 21 per cent of other negligence cases, and 36 per cent of all other cases went to decision. Soia Mentschikoff has estimated that the number of arbitrated private disputes in society outnumber those litigated about 2½ to 1.[3]

The exact extent of the influence of the legal order on everyday

[2] Marc A. Franklin, *et al.,* "Accidents, Money and the Law," **61** *Columbia Law Review* I (1961), pp. 10–13.

[3] Charles Clark and Harry Shulman, *A Study of Law Administration in Connecticut* (New York: Oxford University Press, 1937). The arbitration figures exclude accident suits. See Soia Mentschikoff, "The Significance of Arbitration: A Preliminary Inquiry," **17** *Law and Contemporary Problems* (1953), pp. 698–710.

behavior seems to vary with the issue, the society, and the time in a manner as yet barely explored. Courts serve two major functions in this regard. First and most obviously, they provide a means for securing compliance with public policies, such as those proclaimed by legislatures. Second, they are means of minimizing individual discontent and act as a symbol of governmental concern for the individual's fate, his welfare, and his intentions. Even so totalitarian a regime as Stalin's Russia was characterized by great, almost therapeutic concern with individual litigants in nonpolitical matters.

Courts have considerable latitude in granting individuals access to them. They must balance the danger of overloading their dockets and a consequent inability to settle cases expeditiously against the possibility of becoming so inaccessible as to render themselves irrelevant to the social process. Courts differ in the scope they have to expand or restrict their obligation to hear cases. But the United States Supreme Court is, as we shall see, surely among those with the very freest hand in this regard.

Thus the courts, together with enabling legislation, define requirements for court intervention. But this is only part of the process. The many prospective litigants must themselves determine their ability and their willingness to bring their disagreements before a court. Presumably, some sort of calculation of the balance of the costs of litigation versus the probabilities and possibilities of a favorable outcome takes place in the mind of a prospective litigant. Of course, litigation involves costs and gains other than monetary ones. Symbolic victories may be sufficient compensation, but the nervous exhaustion attendant upon a four- or five-year campaign of litigation may take a higher toll than any financial gain could overcome. People probably tend to overestimate the probability and extent of pay-offs, as they do in picking a profession, a fact pointed out by Adam Smith.

A lawyer as litigant can cut costs and may pursue a course where others would not or could not. The litigious personality who repeatedly appeals a $2 parking ticket may be coping with a deep-seated problem that might otherwise cost $50 an hour on a psychiatrist's couch—a factor of complete irrelevance to the other parties involved in the case.

The society itself, the legislature and the courts principally, define the opportunity for litigation, establishing the instrumentalities and delineating the possible courses of action available to parties. These have particular requirements and skills and resources—the price, so to speak, of action. Whether the price is paid depends upon the meaning to the potential litigant.

These factors are interrelated and complex in surprising ways, rather than operating in simple and discrete ones. The prisoner in jail with an intense desire and rather large amounts of time on his hands will often work at developing legal skills or capabilities. A change in the definition of requirements affects the level of capability and/or intensity of demands involved. Finally, capabilities may be implemented to change the opportunities and so on.

B. The Rules of the Game

These general observations may be applied more specifically to the United States Supreme Court. The stakes there are deemed high by individuals and groups alike; consequently, its requirements for acceptance of litigation have been continuously increased. Nonetheless, like all courts, the Supreme Court must fulfill individual cravings for satisfaction. Consequently, it remains open to those with intense demands who accidentally or through perseverance and foresight manage to meet its technical requirements. There is something genially warming about an institution that decides causes of reasonable significance under the rubric *"59 Kegs of Whiskey* v. *U.S.,"* particularly in light of its general position that even cases involving life and death will not be heard if the issue is not of broad public significance. The Court is a strange medley of jurisprudence and politics, perhaps not different in kind but surely in proportion from any other court in the world.

There are several tracks by which the Court's odd assortment of cases comes before it—representing several distinct roles it occupies in the American political system. A few cases come before it under its original jurisdiction. These cases, limited in number, involve suits between states and trials of public ministers and counsels. A good deal of the latter function has been delegated to the lower courts, and suits between states, except perhaps those involving water rights, have not generally been of primary political or legal significance.

The truly important function of the Court has been, almost without exception, in the appellate area—i.e., in review of some other court's original action. The appellate jurisdiction exists subject to "such exceptions and under such regulations as the Congress shall make." This portion of the Court's work involves appeals from both state and federal sources. Functioning as the federal court of last resort, the Supreme Court reviews cases from the rest of the federal system, just as other review courts do. It tries to set policy for all federal courts within the limits imposed by the Constitution, Congress, and the realities of a common law legal order. It also functions as the highest court in reviewing decisions of administrative agencies. Such cases may be appealed from the district court to the circuit court and finally the Supreme Court itself. But this succession—perhaps surprisingly—is atypical. Appeals from administrative agencies generally follow patterns of litigation expressly prescribed by Congress for each particular situation. In consequence, some cases are appealed from agencies or legislative courts directly to the Supreme Court; others go directly to the courts of appeals, skipping the district courts. Actually, it is primarily at the court of appeals level that most administrative policy set by litigation is arrived at.

But the Supreme Court is also in a very true sense "the Supreme Court of the United States," just as its principal judge bears the title "Chief Justice of the United States," not only because of its responsibilities in the national court system. Under the Constitution and federal laws, cases may be taken from the state courts when issues of federal concern are involved. It is not merely the wishes of a particular party that can "make a federal case of it"; a deprivation involving the Constitution, an act of Congress, or a treaty, must be claimed.

This type of review by the Supreme Court is limited in a number of ways. In the first instance, since it is being claimed that a state is depriving a person of a federal right, it is appropriate and natural that the state first be given an opportunity to correct its error. The litigant must therefore take his case through the rungs of the state system to the highest state court that will deal with this question. (This may or may not be the state supreme court. In Texas, for example, election cases cannot be appealed from the justice of the peace courts that have original jurisdiction and therefore go directly from justice of the peace courts to the United States Supreme Court when appealed.) Secondly, the case is normally not reviewed in each and every aspect to determine who is in the right or wrong. Only one question is discussed: was there a deprivation of a federally guaranteed right? Often, even if the Supreme Court finds such a denial, it cannot settle the entire matter but merely returns the case to the state court to retry the case, charging a revision of that aspect of conduct or ruling that involved a federal right. As the Court formula so often puts it, "The case is remanded for further hearings not inconsistent with this decision."

Before most cases come to the Supreme Court, then, they must wend a weary way indeed. The route is long and tortuous and the pitfalls many. The perils of any legal system and its uncertainties are exacerbated by the dual system of courts in American government, for, as Dicey pointed out, "federalism means legalism."

In the first place, there must be a concrete dispute. The parties involved must be able to satisfy the Court that they are parties with a legal right to sue and that the question is one that is appropriately before the Court. Every legal order has its own rules. Cases coming from the state system must first satisfy local requirements; on appeal, then, they must satisfy federal conditions as well. This raises some problems of interpretation, particularly since federal standards are generally more restrictive than those in most states. For example, "taxpayer suits" by individuals who claim no further legal involvement than that of ordinary fiscal citizenship are permitted to challenge legislation in most state systems. On the other hand, the federal taxpayer who merely has a general interest cannot challenge a federal legislative program, though he may be permitted to do so if he pays an identifiable tax for that particular program. The mere fact that he in some general way pays money to Washington will not be sufficient to allow him to question any legislation he opposes. Restrictive criteria for "standing to sue" is a neat device which allows the Court to refuse "hot potato" causes without unduly antagonizing either side. So, for example, on the birth control issue, the Supreme Court managed to avoid any division on the merits by deciding that a physician has no legal interest in prescribing contraceptives for his patients and therefore no standing in court.

Similar in operation, though quite distinct in legal doctrine, is the requirement that the issue be justiciable. A good many technical requirements as to amounts of money involved and dates of filing also come into play. But even before these technicalities are reached, there must be a determination that the matter is of a type that can be effectively dealt with in the courts. The most familiar standard enforced by the Supreme Court is that the case not fall within the confines of a "political question." This somewhat confusing label— which, as Justice Black has pointed out, cannot mean that anything with political overtones should be avoided by the courts, for that would withdraw them from almost every matter of importance—is the Court's shorthand for a decent respect for the discretion of the other, the so-called political, branches of government. The political questions doctrine is also invoked when the Court feels it cannot effectively cope with the type of question through legal decision, because it lacks power, or information, or skill, or a combination of all of these. For example, it was recently held in a case involving the Nobel Prize winner Linus Pauling that policies on testing of atomic and other weapons are not truly reviewable in the courts.

A decision by the Court that it will not review a certain question is perhaps the most sweeping victory a litigant could hope for, inasmuch as it represents total withdrawal by the Court and thereby erases the threat of a negative decision. From the time of *Colegrove* v. *Green* in 1946, for example, until *Baker* v. *Carr* in 1963, no intervention by federal courts in legislative apportionment cases seemed at all likely. The decision in *Baker* v. *Carr* was held as one of the most significant and controversial decisions in Court history, even though it decided only that Court review of apportionment was permissible. That decision established at least a supervisory role for the courts and forced the states to take another look at their all-too-often gerrymandered election districts.

Some of the standards for federal jurisdiction—e.g., suits between citizens of different states—cut across local requirements regarding jurisdiction. If for some reason the parties prefer a hearing in one system or the other, they may find there are options available, such as suing the company involved or one of the principal operating officers in one or the other geographical location. Under the circumstances, the cleverness of the lawyer in picking the most favorable court and presenting winning arguments on the jurisdictional question can be vital. In recent segregation cases, for example, considerable ingenuity has been exercised in asserting local control under the rubric of public safety in local jurisdiction. Federal courts have been forced to maneuver to maintain their authority.

So, a Michigan case on reapportionment was originally fought in the state courts inasmuch as the labor plaintiffs assumed—as it turned out correctly—that the Democratic majority on the state supreme court would be sympathetic to their point of view. Subsequently, new apportionment arrangements under a new state constitution were challenged. But the intervening defeat of a Democratic incumbent on the state supreme court had changed the balance of judicial forces. A new suit was therefore inaugurated in a federal district court. When the Democrats re-established their majority a year later, a recalculation by plaintiff attorneys, aided by an informal opinion of a cooperative state attorney general, found that there were ambiguities in the apportionment statute and that it would be best to get clarifying interpretation in the state courts first.

Such changeabouts are not frivolous, for the United States Supreme Court has consistently held that it will rule on state matters only after the state courts have fully interpreted the commonwealth position—that is, that federalism means that the state courts interpret their own constitutions and laws in a definitive fashion and the federal courts examine only those developed policies for violation of the national Constitution or federal laws or treaties. If a state legal provision is at stake and it is brought to the Supreme Court, or any federal court, in an ambiguous form, the case may very well be remanded for another go-around, with delay and expense for the litigants.

Thus, the technical rules, both broad and narrow, may all impose severe obstacles to prospective litigants. But even complete satisfaction of these rules may not be sufficient to insure review by the Supreme Court, for most cases come before the justices under their discretionary power, through an application for a writ of certiorari. This is a traditional legal formula involving a court order from a higher to a lower court, requesting the record be sent up from the lower court. It thus signifies acceptance of jurisdiction in a case by the higher court. About four fifths of the cases reach the Court in this manner. The granting of certiorari constitutes acceptance of the case; denial means refusal to hear the matter. Technically there is no precedent value attached to the denial of certiorari, since the judges need not have a legal reason for denial. For example, they might simply feel the matter lacked general importance and find that their time would be better spent elsewhere. In spite of this, judges and attorneys naturally draw broad inferences from denial or acceptance of certiorari that make the technical point of "no precedent" highly misleading.

A number of cases—principally where a state court has invalidated a federal statute or upheld the state law, or where a court of appeals has held invalid either a federal law or treaty or a state law or constitutional provision, and from some decisions at the district court level—come up "on appeal." Technically, the Court must rule on such matters. However, these Court rulings may be based solely on the briefs filed by the attorneys without any further hearing of argument. For all practical purposes, the action refusing oral hearing is the same as denial of certiorari, except that decisions on cases on appeal are necessarily and formally precedents. Thus, the Court keeps quite close control over its own docket, even in an area where technically it is required to hear cases.

The basic pattern of Court discretion through control of the writ of certiorari was achieved in 1925 under the leadership of Chief Justice Taft and involved extensive lobbying in the Congress. In the course of negotiations Taft promised that a full majority of the Court would not be necessary in order to grant certiorari. This promise has been faithfully kept, leading to the so-called Rule of Four, although in Taft's term of administration and occasionally since then even three justices who feel intensely about it have been sufficient to secure the granting of the writ.[4] Recently the justices have indicated that the same requirements are in fact followed with regard to full-scale consideration of cases on appeal, leading to further "homogenization" of the two classes of cases. Thus the Court is much freer to control its docket than at any time in its history and probably much freer than any other court in the world.

The consequences in numerical terms are clear. Something like one quarter of a million federal cases were filed in 1962, of which about 5,000 cases reached the court of appeals level. John P. Frank has guessed that in 1958 over a million cases were filed in state and local court systems, where something on the order of 20,000 to 30,000 were heard by the various high courts of jurisdiction of the states. From this welter of over a million cases on the order of 2,000 applications to the Supreme Court result in something like 100 full-scale opinions.[5]

A study of relations of district courts to courts of appeals by Robert Salisbury covering the period 1943–50 showed the business of the district courts to be mainly civil in nature, followed by criminal and bankruptcy cases. (In recent years, however, unprecedented numbers of bankruptcy cases have created a majority of cases of that type.) But the rate of appeal in civil cases is three times the criminal rate and four times that of bankruptcy cases. The effect is to make the business of the court of appeals primarily civil in subject matter; nearly 76 per cent of appeals cases fall into that category. The reversal rate of cases actually heard was almost identical for civil and bankruptcy cases, distinctly higher than for criminal cases. Of cases commenced at the district court level, the eventual reversal

[4] David Danelski, "The Chief Justice and the Supreme Court," Ph.D. Dissertation, University of Chicago, 1961 (University Microfilms), p. 117.

[5] John P. Frank, *The Marble Palace* (New York: Alfred A. Knopf, 1958), pp. 15–19.

rate of civil cases was only seven in a thousand compared to two in a thousand for bankruptcy cases and one in a thousand for criminal cases.[6] Vines' 1964 study shows that in segregation cases the rate of reversal was significantly higher than Salisbury's figures—45 per cent to Salisbury's 30 per cent.[7]

At the Supreme Court level Frankfurter has suggested that review of administrative decisions has now replaced constitutional law as the most frequent subject of Supreme Court action, though the numerical difference is not a great one. Criminal appeals, only some of which present constitutional law problems of discernible magnitude, are handled with relative dispatch. The remainder of the Court's cases are dispersed among a number of congressionally assigned responsibilities, as well as a number of constitutional areas for court action such as admiralty cases and disputes between states.

C. The Citizen as Litigant

It is estimated that it takes from two to five years for a case to find its way to a Supreme Court decision. Costs, including the printing of the brief and record, are considerable. In the Anastaplo Case the costs were about $5,000, and in the Schneider Citizenship Case $6,500, although there were no lawyers' fees.[8] (Anastaplo handled his own case, and attorney Milton Freeman handled the case on a volunteer basis for Mrs. Schneider.) These merely represent routine costs, not taking into consideration other expenses which may normally be involved—attorneys, witnesses, court fees, and investigatory costs.

Gordon Tiffany, Staff Director of the Commission on Civil Rights, estimated the cost of a single trial in the district court with appeal to the court of appeals and application for certiorari at $15,000 to $18,000. In more intricate cases the costs are steeper. A federal district court estimated average costs to the NAACP in cases "in which the fundamental rules governing racial problems are laid down" at $50,000 to $100,000; *Brown* v. *Board of Education* cost the NAACP

[6] Robert Salisbury, "The United States Court of Appeals for the Seventh Circuit, 1940–1950: A Study of Judicial Relationships," Ph.D. Dissertation, University of Illinois (University Microfilms), p. 195; Annual Report of the Director of the Administrative Office, U. S. Courts, 1962, pp. 89–90.

[7] Kenneth Vines, "The Role of Circuit Courts of Appeal in the Federal Judicial Process: A Case Study," 7 *Midwest Journal of Political Science* (1963), pp. 305–19.

[8] Washington *Post,* May 23, 1964.

$200,000.[9] The comparison by Learned Hand of litigation with misfortunes as depressing as death and the plague hardly seems exaggerated.

Most plaintiffs do not in fact consciously embark on this long journey but rather are gradually drawn into the process step by step and appeal by appeal. But some are congenitally litigious and plunge into causes perhaps with a desire for publicity or out of their own pugnaciousness or ideological commitment or any combination of these and similar causes. Still others—stock brokers, for example—simply engage in activities which involve litigation or the risk of litigation almost as a regular business expense.

The costs are such that individual cases seem to be increasingly giving way to representational litigation. Groups organized or emergent already carry on or participate significantly in many if not most of the major cases coming before the Supreme Court. Indeed, the interest of large numbers of groups has been specifically cited as grounds for the granting of certiorari by the Court. Such groups may participate directly as litigating parties; labor unions, for example, often carry cases testing state or NLRB actions to the Supreme Court. Again, groups may sponsor or support a test case nominally undertaken by an individual. An extreme example of this was *Hammer* v. *Dagenhart,* a case in which the first Child Labor Law was tested and declared unconstitutional. Years later the nominal defendant, Reuben Dagenhart, looked back upon the case and reminisced:

"What benefit," I asked him, "did you get out of the suit which you won in the United States Supreme Court?"

"I don't see that I got any benefit. I guess I'd been a lot better off if they hadn't won it. Look at me! A hundred and five pounds, a grown man and no education. I may be mistaken, but I think the years I've put in the cotton mills have stunted my growth. They kept me from getting any schooling. . . ."

"Just what did you and John get out of that suit, then?" was asked.

"Why, we got some automobile rides when them big lawyers from the North was down here. Oh, yes, and they bought both of us a coca-cola! That's all we got out of it."

"What did you tell the judge when you were in court?"

"Oh, John and me never was in court! Just Paw was there. John and me was just little kids in short pants. I guess we wouldn't have looked like much in court! We were working in the mill while the case was going on. But Paw went up to Washington. . . ." [10]

---

[9] *Congressional Record,* Jan. 29, 1960, pp. 3,663–64; March 30, 1964, p. 6,321, 159 Supp. 503 (E.D., Va., 1958).

[10] From a column by Lowell Mellett, quoted in W. Mendelson, *The Constitution and the Supreme Court* (New York: Dodd Mead, 1959), p. 83.

This sponsorship is not only characteristic of big business interests. *Henderson* v. *U.S.*, a railroad segregation case which helped clear the road for *Brown* v. *Board of Education,* was sponsored by a Negro fraternity. *Weiman* v. *Updegraff,* which established the beginnings of due process in the firing of public employees, was conducted by an informal group of university professors at an institution unconnected with the one in which the affected employees were involved.

Trade associations have long been involved in litigation. Inasmuch as individual business concerns dislike the publicity attendant upon suits, associations may be extremely useful in "protecting the trade workers of our industry." Response to a questionnaire sent to a wide range of business organizations indicates that 31 per cent, as established policy, took part as amicus curiae in such cases.[11] (*Amicus curiae,* "friend of the court," is a term applied to one not formally a party to suit but permitted to participate in a secondary role because of some ancillary interest or because of some information that can help the court.) The bitter economic conflict between the railroads and truckers, for example, which has been in evidence in Congress and the Interstate Commerce Commission, may also be seen in numerous cases carried as far as the Supreme Court. In fact, the whole transportation industry is so highly organized for litigation that different divisions of the American Truckers Association have participated on opposite sides of the same case.[12]

Civil rights organizations have gained fame—or notoriety, depending upon your point of view—for their litigation before the Supreme Court. The NAACP began its long history of successful participation as early as 1915 in *Guinn* v. *U.S.* Under the guidance of the American Civil Liberties Union a number of other minority group organizations have conducted extensive litigation. On the whole, though, economic organizations are the most frequent participants. Labor unions, chambers of commerce, agricultural organizations, and business concerns appear as individual parties before the Court.

The use of the amicus brief before the Supreme Court has increased greatly in comparatively recent times. Prior to 1939 there was not even an explicit rule in the Supreme Court regarding the filings of such briefs. During the following decade the number grew rapidly, and observers both on and off the bench felt that many abused the privilege by filing propaganda or pressure briefs which merely indicated the political power of a group and added nothing to the sub-

[11] Nathan Hakman, "Business Influence in the Judicial Process," 1 *Western Business Review* (August, 1957), pp. 124–30.
[12] *Noble* v. *U. S.* 319 U. S. 88 (1943).

stantive argument. A new and more severe rule was adopted in 1949, though Justice Black made clear he favored more rather than less participation in Court proceedings. However, the Court has given evidence of great liberality in the filing of such briefs since about 1962. The strategy of a good brief amicus is described by an attorney quoted in Vose's *Caucasians Only,* perhaps our richest source of information on group litigation.[13]

I have always viewed the function of the *amici* to take up and emphasize those points which are novel or which if stressed in the main brief, might dilute or weaken the main forceful arguments.

I never thought there was much cumulative force in the repetition of logic by eighteen briefs. Unlike good poetry, repeated it has a tendency to bore. But a weak legal argument, with a moral quality, forcefully presented by an "outsider" will not detract from the force of the main argument. . . .

The *amici* should be providing the arguments that will salvage the judges' consciences or square with their prepossessions should they lean toward holding for us. . . .

The test case, a prearranged controversy for the purpose of defining and settling a legal question, is another method for vindicating an interest. Courts generally look with some suspicion on such cases, for they can easily degenerate into contrived pageants in which both sides are really working to achieve the same end. That is to say, the adversary system under which we operate requires that opposing points of view be honestly presented. Sometimes an outside party can find that his rights have been adversely affected by a decision in a case in which two other parties were involved and, perhaps in collusion, operated to his detriment. It was in fact partially to prevent this that courts began to utilize the amicus curiae arrangement to permit outsiders to call attention to collusion between the litigating parties. There have been many such questionable controversies before the Supreme Court. In *Hylton* v. *U.S.,* for example, the parties stipulated the existence of 125 "chariots" [14] in order to show that a sufficient amount of money was involved to bring the case before the Court. As late as 1935 Mr. Carter, president of the Carter Coal Company, was permitted to sue his own company to prevent its pay-

[13] Clement Vose, *Caucasians Only* (Berkeley: University of California Press, 1959), pp. 166–67. The letter is from one attorney involved in the case to another. I have drawn generally from this source and from Samuel Krislov, "The Amicus Curiae Brief: From Friendship to Advocacy," **72** *Yale Law Journal* (1963), pp. 694–721.

[14] *Hylton* v. *U.S.,* 3 Dall. 171 (1796).

ment of sums of money to the Bituminous Coal Commission. Such a suit would probably not be permitted under present standards.

The courts do not completely forbid such test cases and will allow them even if the situation is somewhat contrived—provided there is a genuine disagreement and the indications are that both points of view will in fact be fairly and fully developed. A purpose of the test case is to bring forward a principle under the best possible circumstance. It is best if the case is what Fuller called "a bridging" case— that is, one that establishes the principle with the minimum departure from previous rules of law. *Classic* v. *U.S.,* which merely indicated that the government could punish ballot stuffers in a primary election, was a good bridge to the decision of *Smith* v. *Allwright,* which held that white primaries were illegal. Inasmuch as both cases hinged on the principle that primaries were elections supervised by the government, the small departure in the Classic case and the surrounding circumstances were excellent in facilitating the much more controversial destruction of the white primary.

The good test case is also one that has the proper emotional, non-legal overtones. An apportionment case involving callous disregard by a gerrymandered state legislature of a constitutional mandate to reapportion is a more appealing call for judicial action than a case involving a recent apportionment by a popular referendum, even though the principal legal questions under the Fourteenth Amendment are the same in the two cases.

Finally, a case which draws support from widely divergent groups is better than one with sectarian appeal. A freedom of assembly case which unites traditional liberals with segregationist groups or the Conservative National Review with the American Civil Liberties Union is more likely to prevail than a case upheld by either group alone. A case which involves a principle you wish to establish but also commands the support of your opponents is an effective test case. So, for example, the American Civil Liberties Union, in protecting the rights of labor unions in *Hague* v. *CIO,* called the case to the attention of Colonel McCormick of the Chicago *Tribune* in order to get this type of unusually wide consensus before the Court.

Groups may spend time, energy, and ingenuity at developing advantageous legal doctrines, spreading them through such media as the law reviews and nurturing test cases before the courts. But the openness of our legal system to cases almost anywhere and the unpredictable rate of progress through the courts is such that all too often the issue is decided by a case other than the perfect one. Even the government has all too often been disappointed in having to go to the Supreme Court with some other set of circumstances than the ones they had hoped to have had presented. The hoped-for case may be delayed or dismissed. Another may unexpectedly come to the fore and move quickly through the various courts, so that the group or the government or the individual is faced with the choice of supporting that case and participating in it or allowing the decision to be made without their participation. At least some government attorneys were unhappy at the "sick-chicken" case as a test of the NRA. Here the smallness of the local poultry operation was such as to make almost ridiculous the governmental claims of regulation in the interest of the national economy. The government would have much preferred to have had a case such as the one that ultimately tested the National Labor Relations Act, involving the gigantic enterprise of the Jones-Laughlin Steel Company. Similarly restrictive covenant housing cases were decided on the basis of a St. Louis, Missouri, case rather than the whole series of other cases which the NAACP had been fostering.[15] The result was that an unpredictable and somewhat ill-prepared local attorney was handling the major brief rather than some of the well-prepared, articulate strategists connected with the NAACP's legal defense fund.

Since the courts are open to individual action in a manner quite different from other political institutions, groups cannot control events or participate solely on their own terms. In consequence, the pure test case is rare. Overinvestment in a case that may not be the deciding one is avoided by hedging bets and participating in several suits, or by waiting for cases to become fully developed before participation.

Much more common are forms of partial participation. Groups encourage and even suggest types of cases to be brought forward. Many decide to support formally or informally cases at various stages of development, including the Supreme Court level. Perhaps only advice and help, including legal counsel or financial aid, will be made available for a case that presents an issue important to the group. In Hakman's study, for example, three times as many trade associations indicated they provided advice and service to litigants as indicated they would participate as amicus curiae—six times as many as indicated they would take over the litigation or develop test cases.[16]

---

[15] Vose, *op. cit.,* esp. p. 517.
[16] Hakman, *op. cit.,* p. 125.

Some of this type of participation is at the initiative of the groups themselves. A developing case is spotted by someone in an organization, and overtures are made to the litigating party. More often it is the litigant, or potential litigant, who brings the case to the group, seeking their support and resources. Particularly in the civil liberties area, group support is almost essential before a case can be pursued, since the typical individual involved could hardly dream of handling the case himself. Well-known organizations like the American Civil Liberties Union become clearing houses for litigation, encouraging and supporting some cases, referring and mildly facilitating others, discouraging yet other potential claims.

The shift to organizational litigation, which became evident by the 1940s, had begun earlier as part of a general change of group pressures in American society. As Harold Lasswell has pointed out, that shift has seen face-to-face, individual lobbying activity replaced by impersonal, systematic, bureaucratic activity. The advantages gained in other arenas are as much in evidence in the judicial sphere. Continuity, organization, specialization, coordination—all have their place in effective judicial campaigns.

A significant force in the rise of group participation in litigation has been the structure of administrative agencies themselves. Merle Fainsod has explained how decision-making bodies often reshape their environment in their own image. Regulatory agencies are constituted to encourage and even require organization of the regulated in order to gain the maximum benefit. It is not merely that the administrative state furnishes more governmental intervention and therefore more situations which could lead to litigation. The administrative unit systematically shapes the surrounding social units and promotes attitudes which can produce litigation. In a sense, the bureaucracy creates an extension of itself in the operations of the political process, and this is rapidly reflected in the judicial process as well.

Whether a group litigates or not thus depends upon consideration under the control of other political structures and the ratio of opportunities versus costs. The decision to go to court may be made because of some special resource or strength of the group which has effect upon litigation or, conversely, because of its weakness in attempting to deal with other branches of government. Stockbrokers, with their strong reliance on legal advice, suggest the first type; Negro groups, particularly during the 1940s and the 1950s, epitomize the second. While business groups particularly seek to affect policy through administrative agencies, and while broad social groupings like the farmers tend to operate through the Congress, libertarian groups have found the courts a favorite instrumentality. Indeed a principal resource of such groups, the appeal to consistency with articulated democratic ideals, is most effective with those who are, like judges, imbued with middle-class values normally stressed in colleges and universities. It is, though, most appropriate that a structure for the vindication of the individual should be the vehicle for vindication of individual rights, though, paradoxically in our complex twentieth-century society, largely through group action.

D. Governments as Litigants

No institution rivals the Department of Justice in its impact on Supreme Court litigation. The United States is, after all, a party or amicus in roughly half the cases heard before the Court.[17] The Department's rate of success is phenomenal, hovering consistently year after year at or above the 60 per cent mark. The Department decides whether or not to carry its cases to the Supreme Court and when it is a party can, of course, refuse permission to others to file amicus briefs.

The Department has built its current effectiveness through careful craftmanship. It has also managed to control, direct, and serve the various political structures with which it regularly comes into contact—the federal district attorneys, the agencies for whom it is the Court representative, and the Supreme Court whom it serves as well as persuades.

The problems faced by the Department of Justice in coordinating federal litigation are largely a product of both deliberate and accidental lack of centralization in the nineteenth century. Until 1870 there was no Department of Justice, merely an Attorney General with diverse and overwhelming responsibilities. With the creation of his own bureaucracy the Attorney General was given responsibility for coordination of the activities of U. S. district attorneys, a coordination which is often in fact difficult to achieve. The Department attempts to control local action through strict directives specifying Washington's policies over sensitive issues, by requiring information on specified types of cases to be promptly reported to Washington, and by requiring Washington's approval for proceeding on others. There have been no open disputes over the relative power of the

---

[17] Much of this material draws upon a forthcoming symposium on the Department of Justice with Robert Dixon, Leon Huston, Samuel Krislov, and Arthur Miller to be published by the American Enterprise Institute.

local agents and the Washington Department; a good deal of local autonomy is still the practice on routine questions.

More controversial is Department's control over the litigation of other departments and agencies in the executive branch of the government. Well before the creation of the Justice Department other departmental solicitors were already firmly entrenched throughout the government; in spite of formal congressional incorporation of them into the Justice Department, these legal officers were long able to maintain their independent roles. The quarrel raged right through the early years of the administration of Franklin Roosevelt. He arranged a viable compromise which is the basic pattern even today. Agencies were allowed to maintain their own legal staffs for the purposes of advice and planning and were additionally allowed to conduct lower court proceedings on their own, provided proper consultation and information took place with the Department of Justice. At the Supreme Court level the Department's monopoly was reasserted and buttressed by its access to information on the conduct of lower court litigation as well. In essence, claims to possible control at other levels were sacrificed by the Department in return for *de facto* cooperation. Once notice of filings is available, the Department's expertise and ultimate responsibility can be utilized in telling fashion to direct even lower court operations. In recent years, the criticism has come from the agencies who feel they are subjected to excessive Department of Justice control rather than from the Solicitor General's office complaining about lack of power.

A primary ally in this *de facto* centralization has been the Supreme Court. The justices have appreciated the care of the Solicitor's work, the parsimonious requesting of certiorari, and the willingness to confess error which have been hallmarks of the Department's professional attitude. In return for this confidence, the Solicitor maintains strict control over litigation and has been traditionally quite sensitive to Court wishes on the filing of cases. Indeed, agency criticism specifically is that the Solicitor and his staff tend to think of themselves too much as agents of the Court, too little as the government's advocates. The Department, however, sees its primary obligation as adherence to the rule of law with an objective responsibility to maintain balanced rather than blindly partisan litigation. It points to its record before the courts as an unassailable answer to its critics.

Before a case is presented to the Court, it is considered by the appropriate division of the Department, and a recommendation is made in the name of the Assistant Attorney General in charge. Normally, the final word is that of the Solicitor General. Both the divisions and the Solicitor are extremely parsimonious in their decisions to take cases to the Supreme Court, only about 10 per cent of cases considered for applications for certiorari and about one third of appeals being favorably acted upon. The Solicitor follows divisional recommendations in the overwhelming majority of cases, estimated as at the very least 75 to 80 per cent of all matters considered.

A figure of major sub-Cabinet level, the Solicitor General's title is etched on the outside of the Department building, a crude but graphic index of his importance. (Almost one out of 10 Solicitors have been appointed to the Court.) The Solicitor may be overruled by the Attorney General on rare occasions, as Soboloff was by Brownell in the Peters case. But in general he makes independent judgments on all but the most sensitive questions. It is estimated that in not more than 10 cases a year does the Solicitor General even inform the Attorney General, either formally or casually, of his conduct of cases. Of course, sensitive political issues—the apportionment cases, for instance—may be cleared not only at the Attorney General level but even by the White House. Of course, one of the tests of a Solicitor General's effectiveness is in knowing which cases should be cleared and at what level.

Because of his strategic understanding of the Court his power has other ramifications as well. The doubts of the Solicitor General, for example, led to the choice of the Commerce Clause rather than the Fourteenth Amendment as the legal basis of the Civil Rights Act of 1964. Many of the questions raised can be intricate and unexpected. The Solicitor General must decide whether to carry the case to the Supreme Court and what position to take from among all possible legal doctrine. Particularly vexing questions are raised when two governmental agencies are on opposite sides of a question or when the executive branch takes a stand in disagreement with Congress. These are normally resolved by permitting participation of another attorney, with the Solicitor General reserving the right to speak for the United States. On occasion congressmen, particularly chairmen of committees, have appeared to voice a congressional view.

Other governmental units also must make choices as to participation, either in a subordinate capacity or as principal litigants. State officials or heads of departments or other branches of state government may become involved in court proceedings.

Much the same relationship prevails between the attorneys general of the various states and the units of their respective state governments as between the Department of Justice and the components of the federal government. But the 50 states do vary in their methods of organizing legal advice, particularly with regard to the exclusiveness of the attorney general's right to conduct litigation; in some states it is actually greater than on the federal level, while in others it is less. Further the state attorney general is not necessarily part of a relatively unified administrative structure. In the states he is in many instances an elective official rather than the personal choice of the chief executive as in the national government. All too often he is the governor's chief rival for political leadership in the state and thus pursues independent policies significantly more often than his counterpart at the federal level. At the same time, because of the large number of relatively minor matters referred to him rather than to the courts the attorney general in most states acts as the final arbitor with regard to a great deal of administrative law.

Local governmental units—municipalities, boards of education, special districts—also litigate extensively. Governmental units like insurance companies must expect legal controversy and jurisdictional disputes to arise. They bear these costs as part of their regular business. In some states local units must litigate through the state's attorney general, reflecting the legal status of such localities as corporations or creatures of the state.

These units and other governmental structures as well are aided in their conduct of litigation by the existence of various governmental clearing houses. These organizations—many of them operated as affiliated services of the Council of State Governments or the National Municipal League—can quickly communicate with appropriate officials throughout the country. Particularly common is the participation before the Supreme Court of state attorneys general, either as a group or much more commonly as individuals. This facilitation of cooperation is particularly important in amicus curiae situations where the stakes are relatively low and where without such cooperation no participation by local units might otherwise be possible. Such organizations as the National Association of Attorneys' General and the National Municipal League have contributed to a pronounced increase in litigation by local governmental units before the Supreme Court.

E. Attorneys

In all the processes of sifting of causes and contenders, attorneys play a key role. Who they are and what their skills may be is sometimes determinative of the results. Kalven and his associates on the University of Chicago Jury Project have concluded that the skill of the attorney is the decisive factor in 1 per cent of their cases.[18] If this figure appears surprisingly small, it must be remembered that in most disputes legal talent is pitted against legal talent of approximately the same caliber, and equal ability produces a stand-off.

If it is assumed that legal skill is always available in the American system—and few would share this illusion—it is apparently violated by the reality. Only in recent years has there been a federal legal requirement that there be any attorney even in trials for serious crimes. As late as 1963 Emory Brownell estimated that 60 to 80 per cent of all persons accused of crimes did not have adequate access to legal representation. The Chicago Jury Project showed, as might be expected, the higher the social class and "respectability" of a party, the better the lawyer he could obtain. Studies of the bar show tight stratification of the profession on ethnic lines, with access to certain types of lawyers and prestige of attorneys equally graded as to the social and ethnic background of the potential client.[19] Of the lower class only those who are actively engaged in organized crime seem able to command top-flight talent. In recent years Justice Goldberg has openly voiced concern over the problems of representation and bail. The drive for improvement of the bail system in particular seems likely to result in success, and the flat requirement of counsel in criminal cases extended to the states in 1963 by *Gideon* v. *Wainwright* should have far-reaching effect.[20]

Generally, cases on appeal have been handled with greater competence than cases at the lower court level, but Karl Llewellyn thought that even so the vast majority of appellate briefs were at best mediocre and only semicompetent.[21]

In many instances, the attorneys who handle a Supreme Court case are local lawyers who originally had no expectation that the case would be appealed to so high a level. Often, too, they have no par-

[18] Based upon notes of a lecture by Hans Zeisel, Summer Conference on the Law of Torts, Dartmouth College, 1962.

[19] Emory Brownell, "Adequacy of Low Cost Legal Services," *Annals of the American Academy of Social and Political Science* (May 1953), pp. 120–27. On stratification of the bar see Jerome Carlin, *Lawyers on Their Own* (New Brunswick: Rutgers University Press, 1963), and the work of Jack Ladinsky.

[20] For Attorney General Kennedy's comments, see Washington *Post,* May 25, 1964; for Justice Goldberg see the *Congressional Record,* March 17, 1964, pp. 5,279–80. See also *Gideon* v. *Wainwright,* 372 U. S. 335 (1963).

[21] Karl Llewellyn, *The Common Law Tradition: Deciding Appeals* (Boston: Little, Brown, 1960), p. 30.

ticular experience, particularly in constitutional law, to justify their appearing before the Court. To compensate, there may be the addition of a more experienced or specialized attorney as the case moves upward to a decision. Individual attorneys will also seek support of various kinds from established legal groups.

At one time there was a distinctive bar of the Supreme Court. Prominent and colorful attorneys like Daniel Webster and William Wirt were part of this era. The attorneys often lived and ate in the same boardinghouses as the justices. They moved as the Court moved.

Today no such condition exists. Literally thousands of lawyers are members of the Supreme Court bar. As early as 1930 James Beck estimated the number at 30,000.[22] Admission to the bar of the Supreme Court is quite simple, and the few requirements are easily met by most practitioners. In view of the public awe admission inspires, many thousands have gone through the procedure without ever handling a case before the Court. The rolls of Court attorneys show 60 names were granted admission up to 1807.[23] Today more than twice that number are typically enrolled weekly from the New York City area alone.

Only a few attorneys appear regularly before the Court. John W. Davis, a former candidate for President of the United States, appeared before the Court just 140 times—73 as a private attorney—and yet was the leading Supreme Court attorney of all time.

There is, of course, considerable continuity in the staff of the Solicitor General and to a lesser degree, since they participate less frequently, among representatives of state governments. The Department of Justice has long attracted top-flight attorneys. Members of the Solicitor General's staff like Robert Stern, or agency counsel like Ralph Ginane, have been active long years and have seen many Supreme Court cases.

Something like a regular bar also results from the repeated participation of individual general counsels of leading litigating organizations. The general counselorship of a top-ranking national organization is a choice position attracting high caliber attorneys. Among current officeholders who formerly served as organizational counsel before the Supreme Court are a Supreme Court justice, a judge of the

[22] James Beck, *May It Please the Court* (New York: Macmillan, 1930), p. 20.

[23] "Attorney Roles of the Supreme Court of the United States," Microcopy 217, National Archives.

court of appeals, and a general counsel of a major Cabinet department.

In addition, specialities like administrative law attract regular participants. Other specialized topics also are associated with one or a few names. Fredrick Bernays Weiner, for example, has handled a high proportion of all the current citizenship cases, as well as cases on military trial of dependents abroad. A few private attorneys, like Leonard Boudin, Anna Fagin Ginger, and John Abt, have handled the bulk of the deportation cases.

An individual with a case of a particular type will, in all probability, be automatically referred to one of these regular channels. To a large extent, both the organizations and the attorneys act as filters—predictors—of judicial reaction. As encouragers or discouragers of litigation, even as instigators of cases, lawyers determine the flow of litigation and thereby doctrine. To be sure, attorneys pick cases they think judges will listen to, but their perceptions of what the judges might respond to is not simply the product of previous decisions. It is also based upon the lawyer's perceptions about what is in the law and what should be in the law.

One need only note the remarkable transformation in the effectiveness of civil rights litigation to see the importance of legal competence. At the turn of the century attorneys for Negroes regularly lost cases at the Supreme Court level on legal niceties alone. Perhaps in consequence, the NAACP places great emphasis upon its legal defense arm (commonly known as the Garland Fund), keeping it separate for tax and other purposes from its regular organization. It secures highly proficient lawyers who have drawn grudging tribute even from filibustering Southern senators. Results have been commensurate with the effort.

Even more dramatic proof is found in the role of NAACP in desegregation decisions in the South. Efforts to limit filing of such cases through threats of prosecution for barratry—illegal solicitation by attorneys—helped intensify and underscore the shortage of lawyers willing to handle such cases. The recruitment in 1964 of a "legal corps" of attorneys, some of them national figures, to handle segregation cases on a volunteer basis illustrates the possibilities of this perhaps most valuable of skilled resources available in American politics.

CHAPTER 3

Decision

A. The Framework of Decision

TO FULLY anticipate the results of a decision process one must bear in mind the rules and manner of proceeding as well as the character of the participants. This is not to say that the rules always determine the outcome. Identical results can be achieved under different sets of rules because shifts of strategy can adjust for changes. A wise lawyer will change tactics, and a wise client may well shift lawyers as conditions of operations change. But no man is infinitely responsive to different conditions; mistakes in judgment will occur. We need not at this time worry about the cumulative effects of such mistakes or the advantages which rules and their changes bring about. Neither do we have to consider the philosophic question of whether in the long run only deep-seated social forces will prove effective while individual cases will tend to be of only minor consideration. It is enough for our purposes to know that in a specific instance the manner of procedure, the type and style of briefs, the time allotted for argument, and the procedures by which the judges conduct their deliberations may all affect the outcome.

All of this is commonplace to any student of social phenomena in other areas. In recent years, however, some observers have seemingly banished the Supreme Court from the realm of humanity and have spoken and written as though pure thought and considerations of justice alone determined the outcome of court controversy. Such a view ignores the simple and overweening fact that any judge's perception of justice is shaped by the social milieu in which he works and the manner in which presentation of an issue takes place. Not that the judges decide upon considerations other than those that a legal system emphasizes—law and justice; it merely asserts that how one interprets justice is a human process involving all of the facets of human perception.

These observations were particularly obvious to John Marshall, third Chief Justice of the United States, who deliberately set out to shape and control the proceedings of the Court. Marshall's innovations were both procedural and social in nature, and he obviously believed both developments were essential to his success.

Moving into a disspirited and lackluster Court, Marshall first changed the form of announcement of decisions to enhance Court prestige and concomitantly his own power. By moving from the seriatum form of decision, whereby each judge offered his own opinion one after another, to the arrangement by which one spokesman—normally the Chief Justice himself—announced a decision for the whole Court, Marshall emphasized the role of the Chief Justice as central to the operations of the Court itself. To be sure, there were occasionally costs for this pre-eminence; as Marshall admitted, sometimes he would have to read a decision for the Court which he had fought in private and thus had to submerge his own doubts and his own disagreements.[1] But by establishing the principle that dissent was basically improper and that the Court spoke with one voice, he helped gain internal control as well as external prestige. It took a determined effort of some years for Justice William Johnson to re-establish the right of the individual judge to speak up in dissent, and even then the exercise of the right was regarded by most of his colleagues as almost treasonable.[2]

In addition to this procedural reform Marshall also moved to cement his leadership on a social basis. He encouraged greater social mingling in a court normally on the road away from home by getting the justices to travel and live together in a common boardinghouse. Convivial sharing even of a regular afternoon drink was part and parcel of his plan. And it was the judgment of his great biographer Beveridge, himself a veteran senator from Indiana, that part of Marshall's success was due to the fact that he "was at the head of a family as much as he was Chief of a court." [3]

Marshall was not the only innovator in Supreme Court history. Many of the great figures of the Court have developed techniques of dealing with cases in order to enhance their leadership, expand their power, or simply to expedite their work load. The Jeffersonian judges sought to break Marshall's control by returning to seriatum opinions. Finally a compromise emerged in the form of a spokesman for the Court and the option of dissent or concurrence for the indi-

---

[1] See *Bank of U. S.* v. *Dandridge* 12 Wheat. 64 (1827) 90.

[2] Donald J. Morgan, *Justice William Johnson, The First Dissenter* (Columbia: University of South Carolina Press, 1954), pp. 181–82.

[3] Albert Beveridge, *The Life of John Marshall* (Boston: Houghton Mifflin, 1919), **III**, p. 87.

vidual. Justice Holmes developed the short pithy dissent to the point of a work of literary art, which indeed found its way to the general public and thus acquainted them with his own dissents. Hughes developed the miscellaneous docket by which apparently noncontroversial matters are disposed of quickly as the Chief Justice recommends unless another member of the Court objects.[4] The effect was to transfer considerable initiative to the Chief Justice.

Justice Black utilized the dissent to a per curiam opinion ("for the court," an anonymous, generalized statement rather than a full-scale opinion) as a means of dramatizing his highly different constitutional viewpoints. And Justice Gray made the seemingly most innocent but perhaps most far-reaching change of all when he decided to dispense with the standing law clerk of long-time service and appoint to that post each year or two with a bright graduate from Harvard Law School.

Social innovations have also been repeatedly introduced into the court. Chief Justice Waite inaugurated the custom of having the justices shake hands at the beginning of each conference. Chief Justice Stone's stern insistence that judges should not become candidates for public office helped develop a further sense of court involvement and identification with what he apparently successfully stamped as the pinnacle of the judiciary. And Justice Holmes's penning of informal and even ribald comments on drafts of opinions helped ease the tension of a complex process.

Lawyers too have made innovations. Perhaps the most celebrated was that of Louis Brandeis when, as an attorney, he developed what has gone down in history as the Brandeis brief. This presentation to the court emphasized not the precedents of the matter but the sociological implications with regard to the desirability of minimum wages for women. (The legend of the Brandeis brief is such that an actual reading of it is inevitably disappointing; rather than being a tightly reasoned, compact sociological document, it really is a rather disjointed presentation of all sorts of undigested facts and opinions. Nonetheless, it does seek to get at the facts of the situation rather than merely listing citations.) Similarly, in the segregation cases both sides used modern data on psychological processes and basic attitudes. The Negro plaintiffs relied upon experiments with Negro children purporting to show that segregation instilled them with a

---

[4] Edwin McElwain, "The Business of the Supreme Court Under Chief Justice Hughes," **63** *Harvard Law Review* (1949), p. 5.

sense of inferiority. One major brief for a Southern state, that of the attorney general of Florida, utilized a sophisticated leadership and community sentiment study done by sociologist Lewis Killian of the University of Florida, showing rather striking differences in attitudes in various parts of that highly diverse state. The first brief led to the famous "sociological footnote" in *Brown* v. *Board of Education;* the Florida brief is said to have been very persuasive in leading the justices to adopt a permissive, local-option approach for desegregation rather than trying to present a comprehensive solution.[5]

But innovations are the exception and not the rule. Most men lack the desire or the capacity to innovate. A lawyer coming into the Court "for this case only" is more likely to hew to the tried and true than to seek some risky pattern of presentation. Further, the rules are already there; they prescribe rather minutely. Departures from them no longer innovate; they become revolutionary.

The same observation applies to a justice as well. He comes on the Court always the junior member of an age-old and awesome institution. There are carefully prescribed regulations that dictate the order of speaking at conferences, the schedule of procedure, and to a large extent the manner of presentation. Sharp departures gain attention but tend also to arouse criticism. Part of the influence of the whole institution rests upon respect for tradition and continuity; innovation threatens that very continuity. Every justice brings to the Court his own personality, his own attitudes, and his own manner of approaching problems. In this sense he changes the institution. But the controlling patterns, the accumulated results of the accomplishments and methods of a hundred predecessors, tend to be altered very little. As Justice Frankfurter once wrote, "No judge writes on a clean slate." [6] The striking fact about descriptions of the operational code of the Supreme Court written by Justice Hughes after his first tour of duty on the Court as compared to the modern picture of day-to-day procedure most informatively distilled by Mason from the letters of Stone is not the degree of change but the remarkable degree of continuity.[7]

[5] A brisk literature has developed on this question. Some of the leading items are listed in Carl Auerbach, *et al., The Legal Process* (San Francisco: Chandler, 1961), pp. 105–37.

[6] Justice Harlan turned this on Frankfurter in *Green* v. *U.S.* 356 U.S. 165 (1958).

[7] C. E. Hughes, *The Supreme Court of the United States* (New York: Columbia University Press, 1928), and A. T. Mason, *Harlan Fiske Stone: Pillar of the Law* (New York: Viking, 1956).

B. The Court's Historic Procedures

Perhaps the most striking fact about the Court is that its proceedings are almost completely collegial. There are no committees and no delegation of powers except for certain relatively minor responsibilities which each justice has for his own circuit. (In general, these are merely provisional powers.) It seems doubtful that a committee system could ever be established; in the course of the fight over the presidential "Court packing plan" of 1937, Chief Justice Hughes suggested in a letter that any action by a part of the Court would not meet the constitutional requirement of there being "one supreme Court." While this letter was purely informal, the reasoning behind it has not been seriously challenged, although of course there has been no occasion to do so.

The fact that all members participate in every single decision of the Court means that the time given to consideration of most matters must necessarily be short. In the early years the judges had little protection from unwarranted pleas; today of course they have considerable control of what comes before them.

Nonetheless, as Henry Hart has shown in an engaging discussion of Court work load, the justices must make about 8,000 decisions in a single conference or about one every four minutes. Further, he shows that if a judge spends an average of only five minutes on trivial applications for a writ and twenty minutes on more significant applications, leaving two hours for major cases including those in which he writes opinions, he will be fully occupied during an eight-hour, six-day week.[8] The Court, therefore, is always seeking more efficient methods of using each justice's time, preserving as much time for careful discussion as possible.

One such method is an increased utilization of law clerks. Today each justice is entitled to two clerks (Douglas chooses to have only one), and the Chief Justice three. The standard practice is for these to be chosen from recent honors graduates of top law schools, who serve as a clerk for one or a few years. Many of them, like Justice White, have themselves ultimately become judges. In recent years there has been some controversy over the alleged influence of these clerks. But the use of some staff seems unavoidable and the method appears well calculated to provide assistance of the highest quality.

[8] Henry Hart, Jr., "The Time Chart of the Justices," **73** *Harvard Law Review* (1959), pp. 84–101. For some skeptical appraisals see Thurmond Arnold, "Professor Hart's Theology," **73** *Harvard Law Review* (1960), p. 1,298.

The short term of each clerk suggests the minimization of staff influence rather the opposite.

The first step in the decision process is for the judges to decide what cases they are going to hear. In the early stages of a decision the proceedings move on paper. Each justice has his own method of dealing with written briefs. Some attempt to master the great bulk of the written material themselves; others use their law clerks. They may devote a uniform amount of time to all cases or merely peruse those which are indicated to be of minor concern. In this regard the Chief Justice's action in preparing and sending out the "miscellaneous" docket—a title indicating relative triviality—is taken as a signal for a justice merely to skim through the case to see that his impression coincides with the judgment of the Chief Justice.

The Chief Justice can have great influence in the organization of the work. There are many things that he does automatically in his role as presiding officer over the Court to afford him initiative that can be translated into effective power. These are minor matters of initiating and controlling the flow of cases. They do not guarantee that the Chief Justice will be the leader; they merely afford him a slight advantage. While many Chief Justices have controlled the Court —Marshall and Hughes—others have been ineffectual. In our own times Stone was unable to control the outpouring of personal bitterness and strong dissent on the Court. Some Chief Justices have been effective merely as presiding officers, while still other figures on the Court were regarded as the strong leaders on the bench as well. For example, Fuller was overshadowed by several members of the Court, though preserving the affection and respect of all and was regarded by Holmes as the best presiding officer he had known.

But the relationship is always a product of the respect held for the Chief as a personality rather than for the power of his office. When a messenger indicated to McReynolds that Chief Justice Hughes wished him to come to the conference, McReynolds curtly suggested the messenger inform the Chief Justice he, McReynolds, did not work for Hughes. In his handling of men, cases, the work load, and even the priority of items, the Chief Justice can sometimes but not always set a tone of harmony, conflict, leisure, or tautness.

The rules and traditions of the Court provide exact guidance for many if not most contingencies. Briefs are filed by the attorneys in prescribed manners and at prescribed times, with detailed regulations even as to the printing and style of the material in the briefs. The members of the Court then move to their first crucial question: deciding whether to decide. If the case comes up on certiorari, the Court must deny or grant the request for the writ; if the case is technically considered "on appeal," oral argument must be approved or dispensed with.

The heart of the Court process is the Friday conference, which begins at 11:00 A.M. and proceeds indefinitely, sometimes spilling over into Saturday. Each justice shakes hands around the table at the beginning of the conference—36 operations in all. To assure secrecy, no outsider is ever allowed in the room during conference, and the junior justice in terms of length of service acts as messenger. Following a long tradition in such collegial bodies, the senior judge has the right to discuss cases first, while voting proceeds from the junior judge up. Since the voting pattern is pretty well deducible from the discussion, little advantage is gained by any justice through the voting arrangements, but it is obvious that such slight advantage as occurs inheres in seniority.

The Chief Justice presides over the conference and has the initial responsibility for classification of matters either as worthy of serious scrutiny or as relatively frivolous. A strong Chief like Charles Evans Hughes can use his power to summarize a case and pose solutions. If he is well informed and respected, his solutions may well control the discussion, whether it be on the jurisdictional question or on the merits of the controversy.

If the conference results in a decision to deal with the case further, the briefs are supplemented by oral argument. Cases are docketed—that is, listed on a calendar—and are normally reached in a few months, but sometimes even more than a year later. Oral argument has become increasingly less florid and dramatic and also less influential in recent years. The Court has severely limited the time allotted to the attorneys; Chief Justice Hughes is said to have cut off a counsel whose time had expired in the middle of a one-syllable word. The Court neither expects nor welcomes elaborate oratory, and the justices feel free to interrupt the argument in order to bring up points they wish clarified, usually within the attorney's time. Some clues to the final vote can often be deduced from the questioning, but it is also true that a justice may seek out an answer to a point that will help in developing his position rather than to embarrass the lawyer by presenting him with thorny problems. It is often difficult to ascertain which role the justice is playing, and erroneous conclusions are sometimes reached from the courtroom questioning.

After the oral argument a conference discussion takes place again, but now on the merits of the case rather than on the question of whether to spend more time on it. Again the Chief Justice has the initial advantage in suggesting disposition of the matter. Nevertheless, the fuller and freer discussion that usually takes place at this point, allows other members of the Court to assert their leadership. Thus Justice Black tended to set the tone of the majority of the court in the late years of the Stone tenure as Chief Justice, since Stone himself was out of step with the philosophy of most of his "wild horses."

The Chief Justice has one additional card up his sleeve—the power to assign opinions for the side he votes with in conference. If he should be in minority, then the senior justice assigns the opinion of the Court. Careful selection of the opinion writer can be influential in determining outcomes; a Chief Justice may choose to emphasize unity by selecting a moderate or to firmly establish a principle by entrusting a stalwart with the responsibility. There is even a patronage element to opinion assignment. Tradition, for example, allows a new justice to select his first important opinion wherever possible. In this way Chief Justice Hughes helped gain the continuing affection of Justice Black, whose membership in the Ku Klux Klan had been given nation-wide publicity, by facilitating his announcement of a pro-civil rights decision soon after Black came to the Court.

Murphy has suggested that the Chief Justice is even in a position to moderate a majority he disagrees with by voting with them if he cannot prevent their success. Since he knows the outcome when he votes, he might well feel the assignment of a proper spokesman the most important result that could be retrieved from a bad situation.[9]

But there are limits to the internal politics of assignment, in that a Chief must bear in mind the law specialties of the justices, their relative ability to handle and write opinions for a heavy load of cases, and the realities of external politics as well. Justice Reed, for example, handled Commerce Clause cases, and Douglas taxation matters. Van Devanter had great difficulty in completing even a moderate number of assignments, while Holmes was, and Douglas is, a facile writer. One of the most interesting examples of case assignment showed the effects of external politics. This occurred when Reed, a border state Democrat of impeccable credentials, was, at Jackson's suggestion, substituted as Court spokesman in *Smith* v. *Allwright* (outlawing the white primary system) in place of Frankfurter, a

[9] Walter Murphy, "Marshalling the Court: Leadership, Bargaining, and the Judicial Process," *University of Chicago Law Review* (1960), pp. 640–72, esp. p. 664.

Massachusetts Republican and himself a member of a minority group.[10]

C. Interrelations on the Bench

Apparently the Chief Justice and senior justices do assign opinions to achieve certain results. Evidence seems to vindicate the impression that Hughes gave himself or Roberts, the other swing man on the Court in the 1930s, major assignments in order to maximize the appearance of unity on a badly divided Court. Black, as senior justice for a minority position on many issues, tends to choose writers with a strong and unequivocal view. Warren has used both strategies. Danelski has sought to demonstrate that which seems obvious but which is in fact difficult to prove—that assignments are based also upon the Chief Justice's perception of the ability of a particular judge. Danelski's method of demonstration—the number of cases written by justices that are subsequently cited in the law books, correlated with the perceptions of the Chief Justices deduced from their memoirs and correspondence as to the ability of their associates—is subject to the criticism of circularity; the results may merely indicate that the perceptions of the Chief Justices were in fact quite correct and that good men turn routine cases into important ones which are cited in the future.[11]

---

[10] Mason, *op. cit.,* p. 615.

[11] David Danelski, "The Assignment of the Court's Opinion by the Chief Justice," unpublished paper given at the Midwest Conference of Political Scientists, April 1960. In contrast are the assignment procedures of the Michigan Supreme Court. There briefs are simply piled in the order of filing, and the justices take pot luck on a rotational basis, subject only to informal swapping of cases if it strikes two judges' fancies to do so. The judge so assigned to a case is expected to become expert and to cover the issues of the cases at a conference. He, but also any other judge, may prepare an opinion, and any opinion may emerge as the majority one. Indeed, to the confusion of the reader, all Michigan opinions, even dissents, read like the official decisions they might become. At the moment of signature most of the judges do not know the outcome of the case but must make a choice from among the circulating opinions. Ulmer showed that in a broad sample of 500 cases the state Chief Justice ranked third in a series of indexes designed to measure relative effectiveness. See S. S. Ulmer, "Leadership in the Michigan Supreme Court," in Glendon Schubert, ed., *Judicial Decision Making* (New York: The Free Press of Glencoe, 1963), pp. 13–28.

Since the Chief Justice is chosen from the sitting judges by the members themselves, it is also possible to measure such effectiveness before and after obtaining the title. In an unpublished graduate seminar paper at Michigan State University Mr. David Wahr showed that elevation to the Chief Justiceship did not, in at least one instance, result in any increase in power. This may be accounted for by the Chief Justice's lack of any important institutionalized task authority.

Nominally only the result in a case is presumed to be binding and a future precedent ("stare decisis"). In fact, however, the wording of an opinion is scrutinized very closely, the arguments evaluated, and the cues thus culled incorporated in the trends of later decisions by both attorneys and lower court judges. Walter Murphy has demonstrated this rather neatly [12] by studying an extreme example, the Japanese Exclusion Cases.[13] *Korematsu* has been cited quite frequently through the years but hardly for its concrete result—the internment of an entire minority group—but rather for its somewhat disingenuous verbal assurances that racial categories "are immediately suspect." This statement—technically dictum, or mere verbiage, obviously opposite in its intent to the overt result effected by the decision—is the real heritage of that case.

Since wording constitutes in all instances a major component of any judicial policy, great care is exercised in writing opinions, and considerable bargaining goes on behind the scenes over the final product. The justice chosen to write the opinion is therefore in a strategic position; it is this that makes his choice significant. The opinion writer often balances the marginal utility of possible additional votes and further assent by other justices against the price of changes in the opinion and alteration of wording needed in order to secure such adherence. An opinion may be broad or narrow, technical or sweeping, emphatic or tentative. Any number of statutory or constitutional provisions or judicial doctrines may be used. All of this is subject to negotiation.

This process of setting forth approaches and arriving not only at the disposition of the case but the actual wording in the opinion—analogous to the function of drafting of statutes in the legislative process—requires a high order of skill. Because of the publicity value of individual dissent and the advantage of coherency and internal logic that single opinions at least theoretically can have, it might well be that even the legal public overvalues opinion writing in the collegial Court and fails to appreciate the behind-the-scenes contribution of the justice who devotes himself to institutional needs rather than solo performance. The reputation of Justice Van Devanter, for example, has risen in recent years as memoirs and letters of his colleagues begin

[12] Walter Murphy, "Civil Liberties and the Japanese-American Cases: A Study in the Uses of Stare Decisis," 11 *Western Political Quarterly* (1958), p. 3.
[13] 323 U. S. 214 (1944).

to suggest an influence barely discernible from the outside of the Court.

This process of internal bargaining is intensely personal and depends not merely on legal prowess but upon all of the facilities of human interaction, including gregariousness and personal attractiveness. Even friendship plays an important role in shaping attitudes although the opposite is probably even truer—that common attitudes help to develop friendships. Social relationships have indeed had great influence; Brandeis seemingly altered Holmes's civil liberties stand, while Stone, who initially was close to Taft and his cohorts, was drawn socially and later ideologically to Holmes and Brandeis. Like attitudes, however, are not a guarantee of mutual respect and friendship. Rutledge embraced Stone's commerce views and was reasonably close though "more liberal" on most other matters, yet Stone regarded him as a "weak sister."

Danelski and Murphy have attempted to analyze further the dynamics of personal relations on the Court in terms of the Bales-Slater notions of leadership.[14] Bales and Slater, social psychologists studying small groups, had earlier suggested two types of leadership: "task" leadership—leadership in the achievement of group goals—and "affect" leadership—leadership in the maintenance of group cohesiveness through good social relations and the definition of moral standards of the group. They found in their study of young children organized in small groups that it was rare for these two types of function to be in the hands of a single person. Broader organizational and societal studies have also suggested that these two dimensions are usually separate. Indeed, some studies have intriguingly suggested that attempts by social-moral leaders to influence practical policies usually cause a loss of their effectiveness.

Much the same thing, Danelski and Murphy suggest, exists on the Court. The Chief Justice normally has an opportunity to establish both types of leadership, at least indirectly. If he succeeds, like Marshall and Hughes, his influence can be pervasive. If he is a social leader and can work effectively with his task leader, as Taft did with VanDevanter, the Court may be harmonious and effective. Rivalry

[14] Walter Murphy, "Marshalling the Court: Leadership, Bargaining, and the Judicial Process," *University of Chicago Law Review* (1960); David Danelski, "The Influence of the Chief Justice in the Decisional Process of the Supreme Court," unpublished paper given at the American Political Science Meeting, September 1960.

with potential task leaders—for example, Stone with Black and with Frankfurter—is disruptive.

Eloise Snyder has also given us a fascinating picture of the dynamics of small-group interaction on the Court. Though there are, as with most studies, problems with some of her methods and data, the general picture seems to conform with our knowledge of the Court. She suggests that most incoming justices spend a term or two marking time in a relatively neutral manner, poised above internal disagreements, absorbing information; finally the justices make a commitment on the basic issues that divide the Court. Once that commitment is made, the justices show great stability in their positions on the broad issues. There seems to be independent if imprecise information in the "gossip" literature on the Court to suggest that ideological and social commitments tend to be made together and to remain largely stable.[15] (However the experience of Justices Brennan and Goldberg, who instantly identified their positions suggests that in a highly structured situation affiliation might take place sooner.)

That the justices recognize the importance of their social relationships is suggested by the resignations of Clarke, generally attributed to unpleasantness with McReynolds, and Curtis, expressly attributed to the latter's unhappiness with the conduct of Chief Justice Taney in the Dred Scott case. By covertly altering the printed opinion to exclude statements made in the announcement of the decision which Curtis had criticized in his dissent Taney lost the confidence of the associate justice. Similarly, when Mr. Justice McLean dissented in open court without giving prior notice, in violation of regular practice, he created animosity that interfered with Court effectiveness for quite a period of time.[16] A good method of promoting task effectiveness is to create social cohesion within the working group. Marshall was the most successful exponent of this method. In more recent years, Taft held informal Saturday evening gatherings to supplement the natural affinity of a crew of men so many of whom he had appointed or sponsored. Murphy calls this the development of a "rump" Court, completely devoid of any "task" elements, at

[15] Eloise Snyder, "The Supreme Court as a Small Group," **36** *Social Forces* (1958), pp. 232–38.

[16] John Schmidhauser, "Judicial Behavior and the Sectional Crisis of 1837–1860," **23** *Journal of Politics* (1961), p. 634.

least on the surface. The Taft Saturday evenings were avowedly aimed at controlling the Court.[17]

The division of the Court into such "rumps" or blocs—whether merely voting coalitions or enforced by personal solidarity as well— is an important factor in Court decisions. Similar points of view in a small group are mutually reenforcing and disagreement painful. Some justices have been noted for their persistently individualistic view of legal matters; others conform more easily. A division of opinion in the Court, usually fairly predictable and along fairly stable lines, creates the framework in which issues are discussed and joined.

If the same group of like-minded justices consistently prevails in the majority, the opponents in minority must shape their strategy to "appeal to the bar of history," expecting to prevail at some future time. If the minority drops below four, it ceases to have any force in consideration of a case on certiorari and thus loses footing. If a minority is large enough, on the other hand, it may hope to gain further adherents.

In the more usual situation of no fixed majority coalition, numerous patterns can prevail. Two writers, Shapley and Shubik, have introduced a "power index" to measure the effects of such combinations.[18] The index is built on the notion that the person who casts the deciding vote can be said to have had the power of decision. On the Supreme Court this would be the person who casts the fifth vote, assuming all participate. Normally, we do not know who was actually the pivotal fifth voter, so Shapley and Shubik suggest we assign the likelihood to the participants in the majority. This would mean, for example, that if six men voted for a decision, each majority justice would be credited one sixth of the pivotal power—the probability of his having cast the fifth vote. If we know the pattern of the division of votes, we can also figure out in advance the probable share of pivotal power held by each voting group. The voting pattern possibilities on the Court are relatively limited; some of them are indicated below, together with the expected power of each.[19]

[17] Walter Murphy, "Marshalling the Court: Leadership, Bargaining, and the Judicial Process," *University of Chicago Law Review* (1960), p. 670.

[18] L. S. Shapley and M. Shubik, "A Method for Evaluating the Distribution of Power in a Committee System," **48** *American Political Science Review* (1954), p. 787.

[19] For elaboration of this approach to the Supreme Court, see Samuel Krislov, "Power and Coalition in a Nine-Man Body," **9** *American Behavioral Scientist* (1963), pp. 24–26.

Division on the Court	Share of Power of Voting Groups
4,4,1	.33, .33, .33
3,3,3	.33, .33, .33
4,3,2	.33, .33, .33
4,3,1,1	.500, .167, .167, .167
4,2,2,1	.500, .167, .167, .167
4,2,1,1,1	.600, .100, .100, .100, .100
3,2,2,2	.500, .167, .167, .167, .167

It can be seen that power is not strictly proportional to voting strength. Rather, it is determined by the total pattern of division. One man in a four-to-four situation has the power of a group of four—or of any three in three-three-three division. Groups gain rapidly in power by coalition. A two-man group would have one fourth of the total power in the Court rather than an expected two ninths. A five-man group always voting together would, of course, have not five ninths but nine ninths of the power; even a four-man coalition in an otherwise completely divided Court would have two thirds of the power and would be pivotal in a large number of situations.

It seems likely that Supreme Court blocs with four or five members find it desirable to maintain the coalition and that, working within limits imposed by their judicial obligations, they make concessions designed to maintain agreement. In a group of more than five the impetus to accommodation probably diminishes. As a minority grows smaller than four or five and thus becomes less likely to serve as the nucleus for a majority, the inclination toward personal expression becomes greater than the motivation to work out joint positions.

D. Studying Voting Patterns

The consistency of voting patterns which we have been discussing has been amply demonstrated, almost to the point of tediousness, in contemporary behavioral analyses of the Court. The most frequently utilized technique has been Guttman scale analysis, although several methods suggested by Louis McQuitty have also been employed, as well as diverse and often more powerful indicators drawn largely from the domain of social psychology.

Guttman's scaling was originally developed to deal with the problem of comparability of responses in public opinion survey research. Specifically, Guttman suggested as a first step toward achieving comparability that items used for analysis be arrayed in thermometer fashion so that a positive response to a question of a certain level of intensity would imply approval of all lower-level questions. Similarly, once a negative response is obtained on the scale, all subsequent answers should be scored as negative. (If you have a temperature of 99.8°, the mercury rises and covers the 96° area and the 97° area but not the 100° area nor the 102° area.) If a body of items is submitted to a group of people and they answer in this thermometer fashion, Guttman suggested, you have a "unidimensional" scale— that is to say that regardless of other aspects of individual intensity, an observer can be confident all respondents see the items in the same ordered way. Items that do not have this quality are to be discarded. In survey practice, however, most questions dealing with attitudes will not scale perfectly with other items. Because of this problem, Guttman suggested that perfection was not necessary if the items were sufficiently suggestive of unidimensionality, that a score of .90 on his "coefficient of reproducibility" would be sufficient.[20] Both tests are simply standards that have been adopted for convenience and have no particular justification either in mathematical or logical terms or in any extensive survey of results to justify their usuage. They are rules of thumb that so far have not presented great problems in their use but may or may not be appropriate.

While Guttman originally developed his method of scaling for dealing with opinion responses, contemporary social scientists in all fields have applied the technique to quite a variety of matters, again without strong theoretical foundation. So long as there is a response pattern, a test of unidimensionality can apparently be applied, and at least we can say that no cogent theoretical reasons for not so using the technique have thus far been advanced. Role-call votes in Congress and judges' votes in decisions are just some of the areas in political science alone to which the technique has been applied. Alcoholism, accident-proneness, differences in types of organizations and union memberships are other areas that have commonly been studied with Guttman scaling techniques.

Such analysis of the Supreme Court has shown not only the general

[20] Methodologist Herbert Menzel has suggested a slightly different test, a "coefficient of scalability" of 60–65. This attempts to correct for the weight of extreme items. If you have an eight-to-one vote in the Court, "consistency" is almost built into the vote; there can be at most a single deviation. Guttman corrected for this by excluding such items. Menzel includes them, with corrective calculations. See Schubert, *Quantitative Analysis of Judicial Behavior* (Glencoe: The Free Press, 1959), pp. 269–376, and Ulmer, "Scaling Judicial Cases: A Methodological Note," 5 *American Behavioral Scientist* (1961), pp. 31–34.

tenor of the breakdown of voting patterns on that body but also makes it possible to order the attitudes of each justice in relation to those of other members of the court. Further, after one analyzes the issues in cases that have already been decided, one can make good predictions of the types of future cases most likely to divide the Court.

The ranking of the justices over various periods of time in repeated scaling studies by different scholars has been quite consistent on the same, and even on merely similar, issues. While extreme stands on the Court on various questions can be deduced and predicted from even impressionistic observation, the rankings of the members of the Court who take a moderate position on many questions are not self-evident, and it is here that the new techniques have been most promising.[21] But it is also in this area that inconsistencies as measured by the technique develop. Justice Clark, for example, has changed rankings on a number of issues. In short he seems to be responding to somewhat different motivations from those of the other members of the Court.

A sophisticated attempt to overcome some of the problems engendered in applying scales in this field far beyond their originally conceived scope is to be found in Schubert's effort to utilize a combination of scalogram analysis and scaling techniques in multidimensional space. This is built on a model of behavior that involves sophisticated reaction to individual cases in terms of a multiplicity of

[21] Indeed, a problem of scaling on the U. S. Supreme Court may very well be that too much consistency has been found. Mr. Alan Arian in a graduate seminar at Michigan State University reported success in compiling a number of scales in court cases by random methods; in no event did he come up with a failure regardless of the random method employed. The literature of court scaling is replete with successful demonstrations of unidimensionality, but apparently only in one instance has a writer reported failure to scale a number of cases—Jessie Bernard, "Dimensions and Axes of Supreme Court Decisions," **34** *Social Forces* (1955), p. 19. (In correspondence she has explained that the data of this failure no longer exists.) All sorts of explanations of Arian's success are possible. The predominance of the small-group influence may be a cause; group discussion of the cases which is thorough and intense may indeed lead to such unidimensionality that conventional standards of significance may be inadequate; the selection process of cases by attorneys and lower court justices advances not totally unpredictable issues but rather precisely those cases the courts will split on in relatively predictable ways. All or any of these may be involved. My suggestion is that the next step for scalogram analysis should be the compilation of a complete term's votes and the calculation by machine of all the possible acceptable scales. Harold Spaeth is developing an "objective" method for scaling that will permit fewer manipulations of the data to secure the requisite coefficients. See "Unidimensionality and Item Covariance in Judicial Scaling," unpublished paper, American Political Science Association meeting, September 1954.

values. This seems to be more nearly in tune with the type of behavior demanded by the institutionalization of the judicial role.[22] He proposes to take seriously and test explicity and directly the traditional judicial motivations rather than assuming by fiat or from meager and highly inconclusive data that all judicial statements are necessarily rationalizations or smoke screens. Just as many traditionalists have often pretended there were no political or personality issues in the courts—though they knew better—some recent writers have suggested that there is *nothing* but personality and politics involved.

Schubert's preliminary discussion is intriguing also in suggesting that purely "judicial values" might not be a constant motivation to the same judge. Perhaps even more suggestive is the possibility implied by his evidence that concepts of the judicial role come into play when other values are in balance or weakly held. At any rate, a systematic study of the relative effects of these different types of influences seems to be in the immediate offing.

Of course, lawyers before the Court are keenly sensitive to (though not necessarily well informed upon) the ideological and personal line-ups on the Court. Gossip about such matters is one of the favorite topics of a certain breed of constitutional lawyer. Before bringing a case to the Court they attempt to assess the possibilities of success and proceed only with those cases that they calculate will create a close division within the Court or a decision in their favor. Since two sides are making the calculation, either both are only halfway correct, or one is very much in error. On issues where extensive current litigation is taking place and where similar cases have been recently decided the line-up can usually be rather accurately predicted within a few votes and the swing men who are likely to determine the matter often identified. Gossip about current attitudes, past affiliations, political associations, and ideological stands all supplement deduction from precedents. The lawyers' calculations are more often than not fairly accurate, whether they utilize Llewellyn's semi-intuitive approach to what he calls "reckonability" or more systematic efforts such as those described in the previous pages.

Courtroom strategies are designed to meet the expected line of division on the Court. Whether the lawyer chooses to use sweeping arguments or halting legal steps depends upon his predictions of effectiveness of one or the other approach. Lawyers have even been

---

[22] Glendon Schubert, "The 1960–61 Term of the Supreme Court: A Psychological Analysis," **56** *American Political Science Review* (1962), pp. 90–107.

known to direct their arguments almost completely to a single justice they regard as crucial, quoting copiously from his own opinions, simultaneously flattering him and challenging his own sense of judicial consistency. Brandeis developed his famous brief precisely to meet the challenge in Peckham's *Lochner* opinion that suggested there was no way to demonstrate that workers were better off with wage and hour laws. Emphasis upon legal precedent or sociological conditions, on conformity or innovation, may all depend upon which justice or justices are seen as the wavering ones.

E. Outside Relationships

As early as the Dartmouth College Case (1819) there were efforts to lobby the judges. In that case personal representations, including private meetings, took place, and a pamphlet based upon the briefs was sent to the justices.[23] We know too that President Buchanan was fully informed of developments in the Dred Scott Case and was expected by Justice Catron to help speed a decision.[24] Today all of these actions would be regarded as lacking in judicial propriety. The tendency through the years has been clearly to reduce off-the-record sources of judicial information to the absolute minimum and to impose upon the justices a tradition of silence concerning matters before the Court, a tradition of "judicial lockjaw," as Alan Westin puts it.

The restriction of sources of information implies that material not in the official record should not be considered unless it is notoriously self-evident and incontestable. Justices may take "judicial notice" of, say, the existence of a depression or a war. Other "facts" of less objectivity should as far as practical appear in the record and thus be refutable by the opposing side. In an effort to convey not only fairness but the feeling of fairness, which may be even more important and crucial to the judicial process, judges have over time voluntarily established ever finer rules to assure the supremacy of the record as the basis of decision.

But the historical tendency of the Court to restrict the admission of parties and to tighten the rules and procedures for the introduction of evidence contract the possible sources of information for the Court

---

[23] Richard Current, *Daniel Webster and the Rise of National Conservatism* (Boston: Little Brown, 1955), pp. 30–32.

[24] See Carl B. Swisher, *American Constitutional Development,* 2d ed. (Boston: Houghton Mifflin, 1954), pp. 245–47.

to the danger point. As the need for technical, social, and political information has become more critical, the Court has therefore expanded its sources of information, in large part through expansion of the amicus curiae device. By this means parties who have a general concern but not a specific interest in a case may participate in a decision and add both substantive and political information relevant to the matter. The growth of the device was gradual, but its emergence in the 1940s and 1950s as a full-fledged tool of litigation attracted a great deal of attention, not all of it by any means favorable. With the placing of advertisements in the newspapers and the A & P Antitrust Case and the urging of the Communist party in the Rosenberg Case that citizens file "individual" amicus curiae petitions (that is, letters to the justices in a mail campaign), there seemed to be a danger that the processes of the Court would become overtly political. Though Justice Black argued for expansion rather than contraction of sources of information, the Court moved by a change of its rules in the 1950s to make it more difficult to file such briefs. The past few years, though, have seen a relaxation of the application of that rule. Perhaps as a result of the change of personnel on the Court, probably as a consequence of a feeling that legal processes have been stabilized and that there is no longer danger of the Court's bending under sheer pressure in reaching its decision.[25]

The partial insulation of the Court from the political process is also sought through abnegatory withdrawal from certain aspects of public life. At least in this century justices have been expected to eschew partisan stands. Members of the Court and the legal public have frowned upon further political ambitions of justices, in contrast to the nineteenth century, when among others Justices McLean and Field were conspicuous candidates for the presidential nomination. Hughes's nomination in 1916 was at least on the surface not the product of an open campaign, and his instantaneous resignation from the Court upon receiving the nomination was in keeping with the modern attitude. While some members of the Court in recent years have been seemingly restless for other office, propriety has largely prevailed except during wartime, when Byrnes resigned to serve as a major administrator. Indeed, in this century members of the Court have challenged extra-judicial service of any kind by justices. Paradoxically, with Robert's service on the Pearl Harbor investigation, Jack-

[25] Samuel Krislov, "The Amicus Curiae Brief," **72** *Yale Law Journal* (1963), pp. 694–721.

son's tour as prosecutor at Nuremberg, and Chief Justice Warren's reluctant chairmanship of the Commission on the Assassination of President Kennedy, probably more significant extra-judicial service has occurred in the past quarter-century than ever before.

Justices are also expected to refrain from comment upon the issues of the day. Many do not, but their discussions are intermittent and veiled. Similarly, off-the-bench criticism of decisions is regarded as highly irregular and embarrassing. A more respectable method to achieve this same purpose has been through friendly use of the law reviews. Starting around the turn of the century, these journals have grown rapidly in prestige and number and today are commonly cited in court opinions in the United States. (The British rule remains that no living authority can be cited on a legal question.) Many of the justices have contacts in the law schools who regularly dissect opinions and trends opposed by a particular justice and interpret and justify those legal doctrines he espouses.

Another force for the molding and evaluation of Court opinions is the Bar Association. Not only do committees of the Association and the Board of Governors itself take stands on legal as well as political matters; in addition, the meetings of the Association provide a forum for individual critics and supporters of the Court and its decisions. Particular justices, like Justice Jackson, may emerge as favorites of the Association, and invitations to the meetings of the Bar Association are often made the occasion for somewhat veiled criticisms or appeals for support.

Similarly, the Department of Justice is itself a potential supporter of the Court. When the Bar Association remained silent to criticism of the Supreme Court by Southern senators and the Conference of State Chief Justices, it was the Solicitor General Rankin who not only defended the Court but criticized the Association for not fulfilling its historical role of defending the Court regardless of the particular decisions it was making.[26]

Do all of these safeguards betoken real isolation from the facts of political life? To phrase the question somewhat differently, do the justices decide cases solely in terms of perdurable principles independent of social reality? To state the problems in these terms is, of course, to answer the question. Political and social relationships are in every way an integral part of the results of any intelligent system

[26] J. Lee Rankin, "A Great Profession Must Act Responsibly," unpublished address, January 15, 1960 (Department of Justice Release).

of law. The social consequences of a decision must be taken into account by any responsible court; a trial judge is not merely a philosopher or a pundit. He must bear in mind his responsibilities to the community and its welfare as well as to abstract principles.

But do justices decide cases independently of their individual concepts of political justice? To state the question this way is naïve. We expect a judge to transcend his prejudices insofar as a person normally can, but we must also realize that judging requires a mature outlook, a standard for approaching problems. It is hardly the absence of viewpoint or outlook that we seek in a judge; the village idiot would be the most qualified if it were. Rather, it is the style and manner of arriving at, applying, and altering viewpoints that characterizes a judicious mind.

These issues were articulately joined and sharply developed in an exchange between Justices Stone and Sutherland in the 1930 era of judicial controversy.[27] In the AAA Case the Court had struck down yet another New Deal measure. Justice Robert's opinion in that case was unusually inept and committed an obvious and demonstrable error of logic. Stone was provoked to attack the decision as one based solely upon political predilections rather than constitutional grounds. He warned that the Court was thereby usurping power and admonished that "courts were not the only agency of government that must be presumed to have the capacity to govern." He called for "judicial self-restraint," a healthy respect for judgments of Congress and the President unless they were an unmistakable violation of the Constitution.

Stone's vehement and eloquent dissent disturbed Sutherland, and he sought to answer it at the earliest opportunity, even envoking a case that nominally had no relationship to the AAA decision. Indeed, if one is not aware of the background, his opinion in the West Coast Hotel Case seems a little mysterious because it answers arguments not advanced in that case at all. The act of judgment, he argued, was sharply different in nature and content from the functions of statesmanship. "Restraint" could not be involved in judging, for restraint, he suggested, involved forbearance, the avoidance of an exercise of power—and power was in no event an attribute of judging. Courts, argued Sutherland, were concerned solely with evaluation and not with volitional functions at all.

[27] Stone in *U.S.* v. *Butler,* 297 U.S. 1 (1936), and Sutherland in *West Coast Hotel Co.* v. *Parrish,* 300 U. S. 379 (1937).

The argument that courts exercise no power—and therefore no responsibility beyond a computerlike judgment of issues—is one that has been advanced by judges throughout history, certainly since Marshall used the argument in *Marbury* v. *Madison,* borrowing the argument from Hamilton's *Federalist Papers.* Perhaps it is only a coincidence that this argument has been advanced most energetically precisely by those judges who were thought to be indulging strong drives toward power themselves.

A more reasonable interpretation of what the judge actually does in these matters is found in Llewellyn's "Law of Leeways." A judge generally feels bound by the statutes and the precedents, he suggests, though to varying degrees, depending upon the individual. He also is impelled by the circumstances of the individual litigants and the social consequences created by the precedent involved in the case. Which of these does the judge follow? Where there is ambiguity in the previous law, he will more easily move in the direction of his personal inclinations according to the equities of the matter before him. On the other hand, if his desire to accomplish the result is overweening, he will find or even invent ambiguities to exploit. This means that the degree of legal ambiguity he needs to satisfy his desire to accommodate the individual litigant is a function of the force of his purpose. One type of consideration will compensate for the other, and the leeway that the judge gives to one or the other is dependent upon the operation of the corollary considerations.

Most scholars of the judicial process and indeed most judges today would regard this as a fairly accurate description of what the judge really does. He neither ignores precedent and policy declarations of other agencies of government nor does he blindly seek to re-create the original intent that too often wasn't even there. Rather, he attempts to blend a sense of historical continuity and policy with a notion of immediate and future justice and desirable policy. The blending is a delicate art that only a few judges manage to master. A good legal opinion in today's evaluation is one that makes clear not only the literal meaning of the law involved but also the policy considerations upon which the case is decided. This, it is argued, does not result in greater emphasis upon policy considerations but rather in its minimization. By frankly stating and exposing their viewpoint to criticism, judges must consider and struggle with and therefore hold in check their policy preferences. And they must also decide when it is or is not desirable to advance their notions of proper policy as opposed to the programs of the agencies of government which are presumed to have the capacity to govern. In this sense, the Stone argument is today the prevailing viewpoint.

As Solicitor General Cox has put it, the Court was not created as a "Council of Wise Men" free to do whatever strikes them as mete and just. But in the interstices of the law there is room for the exercise of considerable justice and wisdom.[28]

F. Small-Group Interaction in the Court: A Half-Told Tale

A good deal of what is ultimately learned about the Court of any particular time is in fact gleamed a generation or two later, dependent upon the vagaries of an individual justice's impulses to preserve diaries or letters, write reminiscences, and commit indiscretions in recorded form. That record is in turn only a portion of reality itself. It is therefore with apologies that the following impressionistic account is presented.

The Roosevelt administration looked upon the Court in 1937 as a challenge to its own power. The first appointments, after four lean years, were made mainly to secure new and reliable voters for new causes. By 1939 after the appointment of some new justices and a shift in the Court's voting patterns, the Roosevelt strategy turned to the appointment of figures who could challenge Hughes himself as a task leader. Apparently, Frankfurter was cast for this anti-Hughes role, while Jackson was put on in 1941 as one who could in time become the Chief Justice. In the interval Black had established himself not just as a strong-minded individual who would vote in the proper manner but as a constitutional lawyer with ideas, and a following, of his own. The rivalry of four individuals—including the Chief Justice, Stone, who had just been elevated—all of whom saw themselves in leadership roles was exacerbated by the personal antipathy of Jackson and Frankfurter toward Murphy.

Slowly, Black came to the fore. He had virtually established his task leadership (and according to some writers at least, a parallel Murphy social leadership had developed) over a bare majority of the Court when the deaths in 1946 of Rutledge and Murphy drastically altered the balance of power in the Court. Reed, who had taken tepid steps toward realignment with the Black wing, was now pulled to the Right of the Court as the Truman appointees came into the picture.

[28] Archibald Cox, "Constitutionalism in Change and Crisis," unpublished address, April 15, 1964 (Department of Justice Release).

The new arrivals were less articulate, less thoughtful, and less concerned about the possible radiating effects of their decisions than were the Roosevelt appointees. But they tended to ally with Frankfurter and Jackson, though the realignment was never a tight one. The drastic nature of this change is indicated by the power index, which shows a drop from an expected three-fifths share of pivotal power of the "liberal" bloc that usually prevailed on the Court prior to the death of Murphy and Rutledge to a situation in which the Black-Douglas duo was reduced to one fifth of the power.

Nevertheless, Black strove to regroup his forces, hoping for additional strength, particularly for Frankfurter's occasional adherence in civil liberties cases. Warren's advent proved significant, for the accession of a third vote for the liberal wing put them in hopeful shape on the certiorari question and within reasonable striking distance of a majority. Warren emerged as a task leader—as had Taft—in the facilitating or administrative end of Court work and at present seems to be the social leader of the Court as well. With Brennan's appointment the liberal wing became the strongest bloc, though closer and more distinct duos remained within the four. Goldberg's fifth vote nailed down a dominance virtually assured by the waning of conservative strength. Harlan's replacement of Jackson was perhaps a standoff and Whittaker was more conservative than Reed. But Stewart was more unpredictable—more liberal—than Burton, and White more so than Whittaker.

Frankfurter's departure not only signalized the coming of a stable liberal majority; it also removed the spokesman of the conservative opposition. The removal of the factional taskleader and the disproportionate loss of power that occurs with the loss of one or two votes to a minority seems at this writing to have resulted in a perceptible liberalization of the stands of Clark and Stewart and the further rout of their wing of the Court. The effect is a clear-cut dominance by a liberal majority that seems virtually unchallenged.

If the Roosevelt Court experience and the power index may be taken as guides, it would appear that a further liberal appointment would probably result in a split within the liberal coalition, while, paradoxically, a conservative appointment would serve to strengthen the foundations of the current dominant coalition. In the light of the present predominance of the liberal majority and the small-group exaggeration of this effect, many of the current, rather unexpected decisions are clearly explicable. Small shifts in number produce great changes in doctrine.

CHAPTER 4

Role: The Court and Governmental Relationships

A. The Court Faces Itself

COMPELLED TO philosophize upon their own role in American society, the justices also provide a regularized, periodically renewed commentary upon the nature and structure of American government. So the opinions of the Court have through history given us a good commentary on both the nature of American institutions and their changing functions. At the same time, they have also provided us with systematic expositions of the role of the Court itself and the general function of judging as well.

It is in times of crisis that institutions, like individuals, reassess their positions. So it is not surprising that ever since the 1937 Court packing fight—probably the most traumatic experience for the Court since the Civil War—there has been serious discussion of the proper role of the judiciary in American democracy. Such discussion has systematically and sometimes brilliantly examined the historical evolution of the Court, its contemporary place, and the possibilities for the future. For some more than two decades the Court itself has been reassessing its place in our society. That reassessment, traumatic as it was, seems to have invigorated the judicial process. In many ways the last few years of the Court have been its most productive and innovating ones. Perhaps only the bitter experience of the 1930s could have produced this new era, for the Court now moves in highly selected areas of its own choosing and acts decisively and positively. The very process of taking stock may have made a more creative Court.

That process involved an evaluation of what courts can accomplish as opposed to what other agencies of government can do more effectively. It involved the deep re-examination of the constitutional authority of the Court in various areas of judicial action. And most fundamentally, it questioned the place of an institution which Justice Frankfurter described as "inherently oligarchical" in a democratic and democratizing society.

B. The Court as Delineator of the Powers of the Nation and the States

The Court early assumed the role of "umpire of the federal system." Its involvement in this area was somewhat imperfectly based; the constitutional authorization is less than explicit.[1] It was first necessary for Marshall to assert the power of judicial review. Once the exposition of the limits of national power was established as a proper function of the Court itself, it was then necessary to find the bases for Court intervention in relevant areas under specific constitutional provisions.

The limits on national power imposed by the Court have traditionally come from interpretations of two key sections of the Constitution. The grant of power to the Congress is to be found in Article 1, Section 8, which lists the specific delegated powers to be exercised by the Congress. Two provisions in particular are keys to the national power: the commerce power and the taxing and spending authority.

Mr. Justice Rutledge once found it appropriate to set forth his interpretation of the commerce clause under the surprising title of *A Declaration of Legal Faith*.[2] Justice Frankfurter has spoken with immense respect for that section of the Constitution, calling it the "great Commerce Clause."[3] Throughout history the justices have tended to regard the reconciliation of national-state conflicts as the Court's very *raison d'être*. Indeed, Frankfurter has gone so far as to suggest that the commerce clause represents not only the motivation behind the writing of the Constitution, as witnessed by the Annapolis Convention, but also its continuing heart.

But, as Rutledge pointed out in the Prudential Case, the commerce clause is not just the basis for federal action. The cryptic words indicating that "Congress shall have the power to regulate commerce among the several states" he described as a "two-bladed scissors."[4] Somehow, from the affirmative grant to the national government the justices have implied a restriction upon the states. Certainly no wording in the Constitution can be said to suggest that the Court is in-

---

[1] A different view can be found in Paul Freund, "Umpiring the Federal System," **54** *Columbia Law Review* (1954), p. 572.

[2] Wiley Rutledge, *A Declaration of Legal Faith* (Lawrence: University of Kansas Press, 1947).

[3] *Secretary of Agriculture* v. *Central Roig Co.,* 338 U.S. 604 (1950), 616

[4] *Prudential Insurance Co.* v. *Benjamin,* 328 U.S. 408 (1946), 416.

tended to oversee state regulations in the field of commerce; yet as far back as the great New York Steamship Case in 1819 the Court has felt that national power was to be vindicated over state legislation by means of litigation.

In its positive role of defining national power under the commerce clause the Court has reflected the dominant economic and political philosophies of its day. In so doing the Court has seen its interpretation of the commerce clause come full cycle from the sweeping Marshallian interpretations which developed and encouraged the federalist conception of national regulatory policy to the present "leave it to Congress" attitude which again shows signs of prevailing.

Marshall from the very beginning suggested that the commerce clause was "complete in itself," as fully granted as if there were a unitary system of government prevailing. When a power was specifically delegated, as in this instance, he thought the existence of the states was a secondary matter.

His successors were less friendly toward the assertion of national power. The Jeffersonian-Jacksonians advanced the cause of the Tenth Amendment, which suggested that there remains in the hands of the states an inherent right to control matters "intrinsically local." Even a power that was granted to the federal government was limited by this necessity for preserving the powers of the states. The Tenth Amendment became a special and undefinable reservation to each of the powers granted to Congress. All one had to do, to challenge the use of commerce power in a specific instance—or the taxation power, or any other power—was to allege that the matter was inherently local. To buttress this position the Jacksonian Court developed the notion of the "police power" of the states and argued that states could under this rubric regulate matters that were properly within their local concern. There being no genuine constitutional basis for interpreting what was "intrinsically local," the justices were free to allow national power where they felt the policy was justifiable and to strike it down where they thought evil results would take place. This remained the prevailing approach from the third quarter of the nineteenth century through 1937. The national government was allowed, for example, to regulate the slaughtering of animals through the commerce clause but not to regulate child labor through the same means. Stolen automobiles could be excluded from interstate commerce as well as prison-made goods, but not the products of child labor.

Since 1957 the commerce power has been interpreted as a broad, apparently unlimited grant of authority to Congress to regulate freely in the interstate area. Certainly the outstanding consequence of the 1937 Court fight has been the resolution of the lines of national legislative power. The Court has retreated from its efforts to preserve a type of localism that had died. Old and cluttered lines of precedent have been overruled, and the clear-cut and sweeping doctrines of Marshall have prevailed. While some may interpret this as a revolutionary development eroding our constitutional structure, it has been a gradual and moderate change, under the flag, not of "down with the Constitution" but "back to the Constitution."

The old Court had argued that just because commerce had become increasingly national and because it was therefore very difficult to draw lines between interstate and intrastate commerce, more protection had to be given the states' rights. This insistence on ignoring economic realities has gone by the boards. "The federal commerce power," Murphy summarized in *North American Co.* v. *S.E.C.* "is as broad as the economic needs of the nation." [5] There is no longer any reliance on mechanistic tests of whether the goods actually move or do not move. The problem is the total impact. "If it is the interstate commerce that feels the pinch," Justice Jackson wrote with characteristic ebullience, "it does not matter how local the operation that applies the squeeze." [6] Far-reaching and seemingly unqualified decisions have loosed congressional power over the regulation of interstate commerce. The Court has held that wheat grown and used on the same farm could be regulated by the national government, on the reasoning that home-grown wheat is in competition with wheat actually shipped and thus potentially a serious influence upon the nature of the interstate market. A retail druggist who sold a number of pills from a properly marked container nine months after shipment, turning them over to the customer in a pill box lacking the federally required markings, was held to be properly convicted. [7]

Not only modern decisions tell the story. The easy condescension with which the old precedents in the field are now treated even more sharply reveals the extent of the shift in the judicial attitude. In *Wickard* v. *Filburn,* Jackson commented rather playfully on "the

[5] 327 U.S. 686 (1946), 704.

[6] *U.S.* v. *Women's Sportswear Manufacturing Assoc.*, 336 U.S. 460 (1949), 464.

[7] *U.S.* v. *Sullivan,* 332 U.S. 669 (1948).

government's concern lest the Act be held to be a regulation of production or consumption," a fear he dismissed lightly as having been
mistakenly engendered by a "few dicta and decisions of this Court." [8]
Time had made solid, respectable law seem almost ludicrous.

Similarly, the Court has moved to restore early decisions in the
favor of the national government in the taxing area and to expand
those doctrines of the nineteenth and early twentieth centuries that
were friendly to congressional freedom. The present constitutional
theory, rooted in the writings of Hamilton, Marshall, and Story,
argues that while the national government is limited to the expressly
granted powers and those functions that are "necessary and proper"
to carry them out, the granted powers can be exercised to the hilt
where clearly applicable. In this point of view the Tenth Amendment
is basically a redundant expression of a general point of view rather
than a really concrete legal limitation.

This currently dominant interpretation, revived in the post-1937
Court, regards the Tenth Amendment, as Chief Justice Stone put
it, as stating "but a truism" [9] that what has not been conferred is
denied. The Tenth Amendment says that those powers that are not
granted to the national government are reserved to the states. But it
does not say that any of the power that has been expressly granted to
the national government is limited by the existence of the states.
To put it another way, to say that "that power which is not granted
to the United States nor denied to the States is reserved to the States
respectively or to the people" is but another way of saying that that
power which is not given to the national government is not given to
the national government.

Since the taxing clause confers upon the Congress the authority
to levy taxes and make expenditures to provide for the common defense and general welfare of the United States, the question has arisen
as to the nature of this grant of power—is it an addition or a modi-
fication of the general and expressed powers of the Congress? The
position taken by Alexander Hamilton, accepted both in the early
years and in the post-1937 period, languished in temporary eclipse
from the Jacksonian period to 1937. Hamilton's point of view was
that the power to levy taxes and appropriate money was an addition
to the other powers listed in Article 1, Section 8. On the other hand,

[8] 317 U.S. 111 (1942), 119.
[9] *U.S.* v. *Darby,* 312 U.S. 100 (1941).

Madison argued that the power to tax could be exercised only in connection with another validly granted power; in essence, therefore, the taxing power was a limitation rather than an expansion of national authority.

Most constitutional authorities have argreed that the Madisonian position is illogical; certainly the form in which the grant of taxing power appears—as one of the enumerated powers—suggests an additional grant of authority rather than a qualification of the other powers that both precede and follow it.

Oddly, there was no clear-cut confrontation of these rival points of view in any Supreme Court decision until 1936. Nonetheless, in a number of cases the Court acted as if the Madisonian theory were correct. They stated that the taxing power could not be exercised even in a valid area of national authority if it invaded state prerogatives. They thus implied that the nation's taxing and spending power was strictly limited to the domain of its other activities. In the 1936 AAA Case, Justice Roberts for the first time overtly propounded the Hamiltonian theory and insisted that the taxing and spending power was a genuine addition to the arsenal of authority conferred upon Congress by the Constitution. At the same time, he denied that the taxing and spending authority could be used outside the national domain. This was demonstrably a self-contradiction, and Roberts' opinion in that case is one that is held in low esteem.[10] In any event, it is no longer followed in its restrictiveness of national purpose, but only in its expansiveness. In a quick series of cases the Court upheld Social Security, T.V.A., and other programs as aspects of the paramount power of Congress over revenue and appropriations.

Particularly with elaboration of the decision in *Frothingham* v. *Mellon* (1923) that taxpayers had no standing to challenge grant-in-aid programs, the door was opened to congressional appropriation without serious or immediate possibility of challenge.[11] The stand taken by the Court in recent years is basically that the congressional power of appropriation is plenary and needs no approval by the Court itself. So, when the Congress decided to return to the states the Tidelands oil areas that Supreme Court itself had decided belonged to the national government, the Court found no legal basis for disapproval. They had held that it was within congressional authority to control the lands, and even to dispose of them.[12]

[10] *U.S.* v. *Butler,* 297 U.S. 1 (1936).
[11] 262 U.S. 447 (1923).
[12] *Alabama* v. *Texas,* 339 U.S. 707 (1950).

C. The Exposition of National Power

The proliferation of grant-in-aid programs has been a vital part of the welfare state and the New Deal–Fair Deal social programs. The grant-in-aid provides for federal government a means of securing cooperation from state governments and local units in areas where the Constitution does not permit direct federal action or where the Congress feels for political or administrative reasons that it is not desirable to have the federal government act on its own. Congress might, for example, provide that if a state will undertake to pay a certain amount a week to its blind indigents, the federal government will pay 50 per cent of the total expenditure. Such programs are very tempting to state governments. Although voluntary in form, such programs are usually designed to make it attractive for states to accede to the federal purpose. When states find they are depriving their citizenry of benefits obtainable at a relatively small cost, they tend to fall in line and agree to cooperate.

This simple account of the practical effects of the grant-in-aid program must be supplemented by the legal story. In the first place, a citizen whose interest is merely that of a taxpayer cannot claim standing to sue in the federal courts. Many of the legal conditions created by the program are such that neither the state nor the locality could itself sue to challenge the program. Even where there might be legal standing, it is the fundamental attitude of the Court that Congress controls appropriations, and judges are therefore very wary of intervening. The reasoning that a recipient of financial benefits from the national government ought to be willing to put up with inconveniences is not the whole story—one doubts that a requirement that all such recipients be Democrats or all Republicans would be upheld by the Courts—but the basic attitude goes a long way toward explaining why congressional actions in this area will normally be ratified.

This expansive attitude toward the commerce power and the taxing and spending power explains why the federalism that exists today is in the nature of a senior partner dealing with his juniors rather than of an equal sharing of responsibility. What the national government cannot regulate directly through the commerce power or the national defense power it can largely achieve through grant-in-aid and other inducements toward cooperation. This is so much the case that Roscoe Drummond has suggested that "our federal government no longer exists and has no more chance of being brought back into existence than an apple pie can be put back on the apple tree." [13]

The effect has been to establish the Congress and the Presidency as the definitive sources of economic policy for the country. Since 1937 the Court has not even attempted to exercise its constitutional authority to invalidate legislation in this area. This deference proceeds from a clear-cut and articulated feeling among the justices that in fact courts are not the best place for the determination of economic policy. The judicial system, they feel, is ill-adapted to handle pressure groups of the economic variety, nor are judges themselves, representative of the community in their economic points of view. "Courts are not representative bodies; they are not designed to be a good reflex of a democratic society." [14]

Further, the justices now see that the Court is limited in its technical ability to handle questions of economic policy. The legal process is such that it is inconvenient to assemble the vast quantities of data necessary for an intelligent decision. The method of judicial operation imposes time lags that can be serious to effective economic regulation. Above all, the Court cannot exercise the continuing supervision necessary for pragmatic judgment and effective control. Its role is confined to making an occasional legal decision. In this respect it is clearly inferior to the "fruitful empiricism of a continuous administrative process." [15]

The Court's deference to Congress is so great that it is even thought better that the legislature be permitted to make mistakes and profit thereby rather than have the courts intervene. Jackson found the antigambling federal tax a system of "taxation by confession," which certainly raised serious doubts of constitutionality. However, he concurred in sustaining the tax, maintaining that "the evil that can come from this statute will probably make itself manifest to Congress." The evil of a judicial decision impairing the legislative taxing power by constitutional interpretations might not be so "transient." [16]

It was Justice Jackson himself, in his posthumously published

[13] Roscoe Drummond, "Are We Maintaining Our Federal System?" **22** *State Government* (1949) Special Supplement, p. 1.

[14] *Dennis* v. *U.S.*, 341 U.S. 494 (1951), 525.

[15] *Railroad Commission* v. *Rowan and Nichols Co.*, 311 U.S. 570 (1941), 573.

[16] *U.S.* v. *Kahriger,* 345 U.S. 22 (1953), 36.

Godkin Lectures, who most dramatically pointed out the extent of the Court's abnegation and deference. He listed three of what he called "disaster potentials" in the constitutional powers granted to the national government that were most encompassing in their possible effects: the war power, the taxing and spending power, and the commerce power. He pointed out that of the three, two are for all practical purposes outside the control of the courts and the third has been subjected to only the most tenuous restrictions.[17] Jackson as a justice and others on the bench have acquiesced in this situation simply because they believe that economic policy must be the choice of the majority of the country and that if the American people should determine to effect a ruinous economic policy there will be no staying them through courts.

Certainly the judges are agreed that economic policy is open to popular decision. The Constitution has "no more embodied our preference for some particular set of economic beliefs than it has adopted in the name of liberty the system of theology which we happen to approve. It may commend itself to a state to encourage a pastoral instead of an industrial society. That is its concern and its privilege." [18] The guard against improper economic policies must be the wisdom of the people and of their representatives in Congress. It is essentially the same answer that John Marshall gave in *Gibbons* v. *Ogden* when he set forward the plenary power of Congress over the commerce clause. The ballet box and not the courtroom was to be the ultimate sanction.

This is not to say that the Court has totally given up all authority in these areas. Even in connection with the taxing power, some constitutional limitations such as those of free speech and freedom of religion might come into play in extreme cases that, happily, so far have not been evident. And as Jackson's comments would indicate, in the field of commerce the Court continues to go through the motions of reviewing congressional action. Though no invalidations have occurred on constitutional grounds, the Court has reviewed the possibility of violation and indicated serious misgivings in such instances as *A.C.A.* v. *Douds*.[19]

Much more usual, though, is the Court's exposition of statutes in

---

[17] Robert Jackson, *The Supreme Court and the American System of Government* (Harper Torchbooks, 1963; Harvard University Press, 1955), pp. 59–60.
[18] *AFL* v. *American Sash and Door Co.,* 335 U.S. 538 (1949), 543.
[19] 339 U.S. 382 (1950).

order to avoid the question of unconstitutionality. The justices thereby have the opportunity to rewrite legislation; that is to say that the question of possible invalidity can be used to give the Court more leeway in expounding what a law means. So, for example, in their exposition of the Taft-Hartley provisions on expenditure of union funds for campaign purposes the desire to avoid the free press issue led the justices to allow the printing of stories endorsing candidates in union newspapers.[20]

Even more significant has been the knowledge of Congress that the Court could, if it wished, once more implement the commerce clause in a restrictive manner. Serious discussions of constitutionality do therefore take place in the course of debates over legislation. The Civil Rights Act of 1964 was debated and adjudicated on precisely the question of whether the federal government had the power to intervene under the commerce clause as broadly as the Act suggested. Legislation is often written with a careful eye toward its being sustained under the commerce clause.

This concern has had some far-reaching social effects in a number of instances. For example, the Fair Labor Standards Act prescribing minimum wage laws was written so carefully that the courts have interpreted the Act to apply only to those persons whose employment "substantially affected" interstate commerce and as not being intended to cover the whole domain of possible constitutional federal action. Whether this was the intent of Congress—that is, not to cover the whole field of the federal interstate commerce power— is a matter of conjecture. But, of course, Congress could at any time amend the Act to extend the coverage.

The process of statutory construction in connection with economic policy is quite a different matter from the process of making constitutional decisions. The Court, of course, affects policy choices through its statutory interpretations, but it is not exercising the last word. The Congress can always overrule the Court regarding its original intent in passing the law in the first place. Thus, the Congress remains the ultimate authority. It is this type of role which the Court has carved out for itself in the field of economic policy—a subordinate role of exposition of what some other agency, principally Congress, might want. It has largely removed itself from any pretentions of supremacy in this area, though it has not formally and absolutely renounced the possibility of reclaiming this domain in the future.

[20] *U.S.* v. *CIO,* 335 U.S. 106 (1948).

D. The Court as Umpire of the Federal System

One area in which the Court retains a vigorous if somewhat muted role is with regard to the limitation of state regulation that might burden or affect interstate commerce. We have already noted the tremendous importance which justices have placed upon this particular aspect of their function. The notion that the Constitution was essentially a "free trade" document designed to prevent Balkanization of the American market is one that finds echoes in almost every era of American jurisprudence. The unique role that the Court can perform in umpiring the federal system and maintaining the balance between national regulation and state regulation particularly through the invalidation of discriminatory state laws is a recurrent phenomenon even today. Most justices have not thought the exposition of national power to be as significant as the limitations upon state intervention. Justice Holmes stated this most explicitly: "I do not think the United States would come to an end if we lost our power to declare an act of Congress void. I do think the union would be imperiled if we could not make that declaration as to the laws of the several states." [21]

There is no provision in the Constitution that declares that state laws that burden interstate commerce shall be declared unconstitutional. In fact, it is only the grant of power to the Congress to "regulate commerce among the several states" that has been held by the courts to accomplish this purpose. This inference from a positive grant of power has some logical problems, and the right of the Court to interdict state laws as burdens on interstate commerce thus derives from what Jackson somewhat unpolitically but rather exactly described as one of the Constitution's "great silences." [22] It is obvious that the ambiguity of a "great silence" is greater than the ambiguity of even the vaguest words.

A number of approaches have been suggested to the problem of state regulation of interstate commerce. Where Congress has acted there is no particular issue; the national power under a granted right, as we have noted, is clearly supreme, and any action of a state contrary to the federal action would be prohibited by the supremacy clause. It is where Congress has not chosen to act that the issue

[21] Holmes, *Collected Legal Papers* (New York: Harcourt Brace, 1920), pp. 295–96.
[22] *Hood* v. *Dumond,* 336 U.S. 525 (1949), 535.

arises, and it is in regard to the problem of interpretation of the "silence of Congress" in the context of the silences of the Constitution that the Court has called its dialectical powers into play.

One theory that has been advanced since the beginning of our national history is quite simply that the national power to regulate commerce precludes any state action in this area at all. This would present a good many logical and practical problems, since almost every aspect of state existence overlaps into the commerce area, and such matters as, say, highway policing would become difficult under any notion of the exclusive authority of the national government. Another theory suggests that where the Congress has not acted, the states ought to be completely free to regulate; thus the Court ought not intervene where Congress has not chosen to assert national authority. These two extremes have one thing in common: they would leave to the Court a minor role in defending internal commerce and the federal system.

The notion that the states ought to be free to act in the field of interstate commerce unless Congress finds fault with their actions or has some affirmative policy of its own has not generally found favor with students of the American federal system. They point out that most burdens by state legislation on interstate commerce are relatively minor; they are not dramatic events but rather small bits of legislation—a regulation of milk production, the special tax levied on colored oleo, a discriminatory tax on outside trucking firms, and matters of this sort. Individually they are of no great moment; *in toto* they present a real problem. To wait for Congress to remedy the situation would usually be to wait in vain, for an overburdened national legislature is unlikely even to notice such small incidents until an established pattern of discrimination prevails throughout the country. The probable solution would then not be the sweeping away of state regulations but some sort of a political compromise that would allow their continuation.

On the other hand, the Court can deal with these cases as they come up. Individuals must, of course, take initiative and bring forward cases, but it is often well worth their while to go through the legal process because large sums of money are usually involved. Such cases dealing with minute legal detail are precisely the type of consideration the judges are best prepared to handle.

Thus, practical political considerations, the needs of the nation, and the specialties of the Court have all combined to suggest that the field of interstate regulation and taxation should be a legal matter. And in spite of occasional outcries after particular decisions, and even though the Supreme Court has never succeeded in articulating a simple, uniform standard for the treatment of all state efforts to regulate interstate commerce, there have been relatively few sustained attempts to remove the Court from this particular area.

The Court maintains its particularly active role in ruling on state regulation because it has rejected both the notion' that the states may never regulate interstate commerce and that they may do so freely unless Congress acts. Instead, the Court decides cases under some sort of variation of the 1852 "Cooley rule." That rule developed out of legislation by Pennsylvania which, by setting extra fees for pilots not licensed in Pennsylvania, encouraged the use of local pilots. Because there was also a federal licensing act, there was some question whether Pennsylvania could regulate in the field of navigation at all. The Court decided that the legislation was constitutional. It divided the entire area of interstate commerce into several parts. Where congressional action precluded state regulation, federal supremacy would prevail. If there were no conflicting federal legislation—and they held that the congressional act did not conflict in this instance—then the Court had to decide whether or not to sustain the state statute. States could act so long as the matter involved was of a local nature and did not require a national rule. If it was of such a nature that one national policy was required—even if Congress had failed to provide that policy—no state could legislate. Further, a state might not burden interstate commerce to the point of limiting its flow.[23]

In view of the fact that, as Calvin Coolidge pointed out to us so cogently, "the business of America is business," the field of interstate regulation has provided the occasion for many a lawyer to exercise his ingenuity. This ingenuity has brought a whole host of doctrines and arguments about when a state might regulate and when not. The Court has not been above inventing special doctrines for a particular case and then being faced with the problem of doing something with the precedent. As the court opinion in *Freeman* v. *Hewitt* suggested, "to attempt to harmonize all that has been said in the past would neither clarify what has gone before nor guide the future" in the field of interstate commerce regulation.[24] But in general it is fair to say that the various doctrines that have been used in the century since the formulation of the Cooley rule have been variations of its essential formula.

[23] *Cooley* v. *Bd. of Wardens,* 12 How. 299 (1852).

[24] 329 U.S. 249 (1946), 252.

The Court today will generally sustain state legislation on interstate commerce if it does not violate certain highly specific restrictions; this represents an expansion of state authority that was accomplished by the Roosevelt Court and its successors, during an era in which in other areas the Court generally restricted state control. Such expansion of states rights in the field of economic policy is often overlooked by critics of the United States Supreme Court who see only a diminution of state power in our time.

There remain restrictions on state control over interstate commerce however. A tax or regulation that is patently discriminatory against interstate commerce is viewed with considerable suspicion. Efforts to keep out competing products from other states are regarded as vulnerable to attack. Yet the deference that the Court will pay to state legislatures and their unwillingness to impute such motives to them means that it is always doubtful that such statutes will be overruled. Similarly, where there exists the threat of "multiple burdens"—that is, the possibility of continued exaction of taxes on the same product by state after state to the point of discouragement of interstate commerce—the Court might very well intervene. These rules are not exact or wholly consistent, however, and it is fair to say, as one eminent writer on the subject has observed, that "one must conclude that interstate commerce today is both overprotected in some instances and underprotected in others." [25]

It would appear that the general guide on deciding questions on the validity of state laws remains essentially the test suggested by Chief Justice Stone in many opinions, the "balancing of interests." This he regarded as part of a new tendency in American law to view nation and state not as competing authorities but as mutually reinforcing and supplementary aspects of social power. He thought the Court ought to try to reconcile and accommodate the national and state authorities and to permit both to regulate wherever possible. Thus, even the existence of a federal law did not necessarily mean that the state was precluded from action in a certain field of regulation if there was no contradiction between the purposes and general philosophy of the federal statute and the exact provisions of the state law. Where there was no direct collision but only a generalized threat to federal authority, he suggested that the federal supremacy should not be absolute. Rather, the Court ought to weigh the general advantages of federal and state involvement.

The "balancing of interests" approach implies frankly an arbiter's

[25] Herbert Weinstock, "Why Exempt Interstate Commerce?" **19** *George Washington Law Review* (1951), pp. 613–14.

role for the Supreme Court. The justices are to arrive at their disposition of authority not on the basis of any legal formula but on its assessment of which level of government can best accomplish the purpose. Also taken into account are the costs to society of exclusively allocating a matter to federal authority as against permitting the state to regulate.

How can the Court justify its striking down of state regulations in interstate commerce, thus affecting economic policy? Is there not a discrepancy between its stand here and its position on the exposition of national power? Part of the answer lies in the spirit implicit in Holmes's notion that to preserve the nation as a nation someone must have the authority to invalidate separatist state laws.

But for greater consistency the Court has attempted to deemphasize its power by expanding and making more prominent the general formula known as the Webb-Kenyon principle. Presumably, if a state law is declared a burden on interstate commerce either because of its discriminatory nature or because of the need for a uniform national policy, it is the Constitution as implemented by the Court that is made the basis for striking down the state law. What happens then if Congress expressly permits the state to do that which the Court had declared forbidden by the Constitution? On logical grounds it might be argued that the Court should not permit such an action. If a constitutional provision forbade the states from acting, then seemingly no act of Congress could permit them to do so. But in fact the Court has for a long period of time been rather more lenient on this.

The permission given by Congress to the states in the nineteenth century to prohibit the interstate shipment of liquor was upheld by the Court even though the justices had previously held that no state had such a power. Since then the Congress has acted in this vein in a number of different areas. States are in effect permitted by act of Congress to use congressional powers in order to accomplish something which otherwise they might not constitutionally be able to do. The Court has been increasingly lenient with state legislation and taxation of interstate commerce; but if the Congress does not agree with the Court's evaluation of the desirability of the state legislation it is not stymied. It may permissively through direct legislation permit the states to regulate. Thus, although the Court acts as a constitutional agent, it has provided a means whereby the Congress is the final arbiter. The Court's function here is not very different from its function of normal statutory interpretation in that it does not have the last word.

Indeed, what many regard as the most important area of Court authority in the field of interstate commerce is but an expanded aspect of statutory interpretation. When there is direct confrontation of a federal and a state statute, the federal, of course, must prevail. But what is meant by direct confrontation of two statutes? Laws very seldom say exactly and completely the opposite of each other. Yet two laws may seem to be about entirely different matters and yet come into direct collision. For example, a national labor regulation might conflict with a corporation registration requirement on the state level in such a way that either the unions or the business might not be able to comply with certain aspects of both laws. In practice, whether or not there is a contradiction between two statutes is subject to interpretation by judges. That interpretation is largely a question of the intent of the legislature.

In recent years the Court has used an aspect of this ambiguity in a more expansive way. Sometimes a federal statute will provide for a plan that by its very nature excludes state action, though the law does not clearly state this to be the case. For example, a good deal of labor union procedure prescribed on the national level suggests that states cannot do certain things that are contrary to the spirit of the congressional actions. If state judges could issue injunctions on matters otherwise in the hands of the NLRB, little coordination of policy by that agency would be possible.

As broader regulatory statutes become more common on the federal level, the Court has had to declare more and more often that a specific state act is prohibited by a general federal statute that has "occupied the field" to the exclusion of the state action. In a sense we have here an application of a form of the Cooley rule: where there appears to be, through congressional action, an attempt to create one broad national uniform policy, no local intervention will be permitted. When the Court declares that Congress has "occupied a field" or that "supersedure" of the area by federal legislation has taken place, it effectively prevents state action much as it would on a constitutional basis. But here explicitly—and somewhat more logically—Congress has the power to overrule the Court. That is, it can always state by new legislation that there was no intent to occupy the field or pre-empt the state from any action.

The practice of the Court invalidating state laws on pre-emption grounds has been so common that Congress has adopted a device to counter the Court's influence. It is now standard practice for many congressional acts to include a provision that there is no intention to preclude state action in the area. This "antipreemption" device is intended to limit the Court's intervention, but the technical problems of statutory construction are such that even this does not totally preclude the possibility that the Court will find an intent to pre-empt. While they may rule that the statute as a whole does not pre-empt the domain of the whole act, there may be found an intention to occupy some small aspect of the field by federal law alone. This puts a premium on very clever draftsmanship on the part of the Congress.

In interstate commerce all three members of the state-Congress-Court triangle have had some advantages accruing to them in recent years. The Court, satisfied that this is an important area for the judicial process, has moved more into the area of statutory construction, making it amply clear, however, that it accepts the overriding control of Congress. In turn, Congress is now enhanced both with respect to its clear-cut authority over reassignment of power to the states (even after they had been prohibited from exercising authority) and insofar as the pre-emption of the field technique has become more common. It has not really eliminated the Court as the day-to-day controller of the question simply because it has not been technically feasible for Congress to take over the area. A 1964 study by the House Interstate Commerce Committee has suggested more comprehensive legislation, a suggestion that probably would be welcomed by the Court. While the states now are subject to control both by the courts and Congress, it is simply a fact that the courts of the 1950s and 1960s are incomparably more tolerant of state action than they were in the 1930s.

E. The Court as Overseer of the Separation of Powers

At times American government seems to magnify Brandeis's claim that "the purpose of the separation of powers was, not to avoid friction, but by the means of the inevitable friction . . . to save the people from autocracy." [26] Day-to-day turmoil sometimes suggests that the conflict *is* the end and that the system exists for the sake of the controversy. In this area the Court has played a significant role, usually as a mediator. Controversies of this type are what George Wharton Pepper [27] has styled "family quarrels," involving such matters as the appointment of executive officials, the treatymaking power,

[26] *Myers* v. *U.S.,* 272 U.S. 52 (1926), 3.
[27] G. W. Pepper, *Family Quarrels* (New York: Baker, Voorhis and Co., 1931).

and the domain of congressional inquiry over executive matters. Most recently, the Court has accepted responsibility for exercising control over the apportionment question in American politics.

These are all areas of great delicacy and possible turmoil. The Court has not usually sought out nor particularly welcomed challenges between branches of government, even when the conflict was between the President and the Congress. It was precisely to avoid such enbroilment that the Court developed one of the vaguest and most intriguing of its rules, its observation that it would not deal with "political questions." This comes close to Stone's notion of the scope of "judicial self-restraint." No one has summarized the political questions doctrine better than John P. Frank. He sees four elements involved in Court evaluation of a matter as a political question; "the need of quick and single policy," "judicial incompetence," "clear prerogative of another branch of government," and "avoidance of unmanageable situations." [28]

The political questions doctrine, however, does not mean that anything that is tinged with politics or even that any matter that might properly fall within the domain of the President or the Congress shall not be reviewable, for that would end the whole constitutional function of the Court. In a good many of these areas indeed, the judges have gained new confidence and have moved to assert more power rather than less.

The recent redefinition of the Court role has been most instructive in the area of separation of powers. The Court has clearly been more active on questions of removal of executive employees. The first such question that faced the Court was the problem of the general removal power of the President over his subordinates. In 1926 in the Myers Case a sweeping decision by Chief Justice Taft, himself a former President, suggested that the President could remove anyone he appointed through the normal channels of Senate confirmation for any reasons he chose. Holmes observed at the time that Brandeis's dissent demonstrated that the arguments of Taft were mere "spider webs" incapable of supporting the doctrine Taft sought to assert and were bound to fail.[29]

This prediction seems to have been well borne out in that in the Humphrey Case and more recently in the Weiner Case the Court

---

[28] John P. Frank and Edmond Cahn, *Supreme Court and Supreme Law* (Bloomington: Indiana University Press, 1954), pp. 36–47.

[29] *Myers* v. *U.S.*, 272 U.S. 52 (1926), 177.

has severely limited the President's right to remove subordinates.[30] It is only "purely executive" officials for whom the President retains his right of removal, but those who are in "quasi-legislative" and "quasi-judicial" positions are not removable by the President except for reasons specified by Congress.

The Court has not yet developed very complete notions of what are in fact "quasi-legislative" and "quasi-judicial" positions, but to do so will provide them with a good deal more authority in the future. Certainly it is the Congress that has been most enhanced in its potential disagreements with the President. Presumably, the domain of nonexecutive officials who serve the Presidency is relatively limited to those who in fact do make some kind of awards and determinations of a semijudicial nature. (In *Morgan* v. *TVA,* on the other hand, the Court refused to review the removal of a member of a commission who had made unsupported charges against another member of the same body, even though this was not an explicit grounds for removal under the congressional statute.[31] It is possible that the TVA was thus held by the Court in effect not to be such a semi-ajudicatory organization.)

A second major question, never long out of newspaper headlines, concerns the removal of lesser bureaucrats for security reasons. This controversial area has split the Court for many years now. A good many decisions on this matter have been written by shifting majorities, with changes of personnel of one or two members radically affecting the stand of the Court. For that reason, it is particularly difficult to draw generalizations in this area. But in the last 20 years or so the Court has pretty well established the principle that governmental employees are entitled to some sort of judicial protection prior to their removal. The older stand had been that governmental employment was clearly a privilege and therefore any reasons for removal were valid. "The petitioner may have a constitutional right to talk politics," Justice Holmes, then of the Massachusetts court, explained, "but he has no constitutional right to be a policeman." [32] Such a simple approach to the problem was unlikely to prevail in a society in which one out of seven workers was employed by a governmental authority. Today, among other grounds for judicial reversal

[30] *Humphrey* v. *U.S.,* 295 U.S. 602 (1935); *Weiner* v. *U.S.,* 357 U.S. 349 (1958).
[31] *Morgan* v. *TVA,* 312 U.S. 701 (1941).
[32] *McAullife* v. *Mayor of New Bradford,* 155 Mass. 216 (1892), 220.

of removal of government employees has been the failure to provide a hearing on charges, a change by the agency of its own procedures for removal in the middle of the hearing, and the use of a presidential order rather than a congressional statute to establish procedures of firing. All of this has meant an increase in the importance of the Court.

In the field of foreign affairs the Court has developed a more definite doctrine. On the one hand, it has tried to develop a domain of exclusive executive prerogatives; on the other hand, it has made clear that not even the needs of foreign affairs and national security exempt the executive from obedience to clear-cut constitutional requirements such as those embodied in the Bill of Rights.

The Court has consistently ruled that the executive is the sole spokesman of the United States in foreign affairs. This emerges clearly in a number of cases ranging from the famous *U.S.* v. *Pink,* involving the recognition of the Soviet Union and the assignment of property rights within the United States to the Soviet government,[33] to the decision indicating that the courts had no authority over the confiscation of property in Cuba and such cases as *Chicago and Southern Airlines* v. *Waterman Steamship Corporation,* involving presidential and CAB directives establishing international air routes.[34] In general, the Court will grant a wide berth to executive action where foreign policy expertise might be involved, where there is a need for a single voice and a uniform policy, as in the recognition of a country, or where the risks of court decision are too great. The Japanese Exclusion Cases, involving a question of national safety, show how far the Court has gone in recognizing executive prerogatives, even to an extent now generally admitted to have been an error.

But the Court has in recent years also introduced limitations upon the foreign policy scope of the executive and the extent to which the President may alter domestic law by foreign agreements. In part this has come about due to the agitation over the scope of treaties and executive agreements that led to the formulation of proposals known as the Bricker amendment.

Two key decisions in the 1920s and 1930s had suggested that the scope of executive and congressional action in foreign affairs was not limited by the Constitution. In *Missouri* v. *Holland* [35] Justice

[33] 315 U.S. 203 (1942).
[34] 333 U.S. 103 (1948).
[35] 252 U.S. 416 (1920).

Holmes suggested that it was doubtful that there were any limitations on the presidential treaty-making power except the requirement that a treaty be approved by the Senate. In *U.S.* v. *Curtiss-Wright Export Corporation* [36] Justice Sutherland distinguished between the domain of the Constitution in domestic affairs and in foreign matters. Sutherland, who had lectured on this favorite topic of his before going on the Court, indicated that the President had an untrammeled voice in foreign affairs and was essentially above the Constitution in this area.[37] The Curtiss-Wright decision also for the first time gave judicial approval to the position that executive agreements, which are treatylike arrangements with foreign countries that do not have the approval of the Senate, are nonetheless the law of the land and are enforceable in court action. They are in fact the equal of domestic law as treaties are with the only test of which prevails being which is the latest that is promulgated.

Critics of both decisions pointed out that the effect would not only be to allow the President and the Senate combined to change the law of the United States but also to give the President alone that power via executive agreement. Since there was no clear-cut limitation, the President might negotiate almost any arrangement with a foreign country and claim that our domestic law was thereby altered. This resulted in the proposals of Senator Bricker to limit the executive agreement power by constitutional amendment and require Senate approval of such agreements, as well as to provide that treaties must conform with the Constitution of the United States. The severe technical problems that the proposal engendered resulted in a whole series of amendments, offered in the name of "the Bricker amendment." For many years the proposal drew substantial support in the House and Senate and very nearly secured passage even though opposed both by the dominant wing of the Democratic party and by the Eisenhower administration itself.

Perhaps in response to this agitation, but at any rate acting to allay fears and to end agitation for such proposals, the Court subsequently made it clear that there are limitations upon the presidential treatymaking power. In a case involving a treaty with Canada that in effect allowed the Senate alone to dictate disposition of electric

[36] 294 U.S. 304 (1936).
[37] President Roosevelt himself thought the decision strained, that the constitutional provisions "do not go nearly as far as the decisions of the Supreme Court in interpreting that language." *The Inside Struggle,* Vol. II of *The Secret Diary of Harold Ickes* (New York: Simon and Schuster, 1954), p. 637.

power produced solely within the United States—a provision that was put in by the Senate without regard to any of the wishes of Canada— the courts have ruled that a treaty must be limited to a valid *foreign* purpose. It is obvious that the Court will be the one to have the final say as to whether such a valid purpose exists. Similarly, in a case involving servicemen's dependents abroad with the armed forces, the Supreme Court held that the mere existence of a treaty with a foreign country did not provide the military with a basis for holding civilians and trying them under military law. The treaty power was thus limited by the constitutional provisions with regard to a jury trial and domestic civilian control.[38]

The most dramatic assertion of Court power and denial of executive action came in the famous Steel Seizure Case.[39] President Truman had intervened in a labor-management dispute to avert shortages of military supplies in the Korean "police action," citing also the need for fulfillment of commitments to NATO and other allies. While citing his responsibilities as Commander in Chief of the Armed Forces, he relied generally upon the inherent powers of the executive above and beyond those specified in the Constitution itself. The justices were disturbed by the consequence of allowing the executive to claim an enlargement of his domestic powers as a consequence of a foreign situation which he had himself created without any declaration of war or authorization from the Congress. But this was a factor lurking behind the scenes rather than an acknowledged basis of the opinions. Officially, the badly divided court—six opinions in all were written—insisted that the President did not have the authority to circumvent congressionally established means of dealing with the problem. Even though the President might have had inherent powers to deal with the situation in the absence of any congressional legislation, the fact that the President could have dealt with this labor emergency through the machinery established by no less than two congressional acts precluded his resorting to the claim of inherent power.

In short, if the President did not wish to follow the routes opened to him by Congress, he had to accept the consequences and could not claim an emergency power. The justices justified their denial of authority to the Presidency on the grounds that the Congress had spoken. In this respect, *Youngstown Sheet and Tube* v. *Sawyer,* the

[38] *Reid* v. *Covert,* 351 U.S. 487 (1956); *Power Authority of New Work* v. *FPC,* 247 F.2d 538 (1957).
[39] *Steel Seizure Case,* 343 U.S. 579 (1952).

steel seizure case, is a paradigmatic case that reflects the tendency of the Court to question most severely the actions of an agency of one of the two cognate branches of government if the other is opposed; on the other hand, where President and Congress are in agreement, the Court is not likely to invalidate their actions.

An important illustration of this has been the recent Court acceptance of authority to deal with the problem of legislative apportionment. There had been relatively few such cases before the Court prior to the decision of *Colegrove* v. *Green* in 1946, and those decisions had been on the whole ambiguous. In 1946, however, in answer to a challenge to the Illinois congressional apportionment a four-to-three majority determined that no reapportionment was to take place. While Justice Rutledge, who cast the deciding vote, did so on grounds of immediate equitable considerations rather than on the basic issue, Frankfurter's opinion suggested that such a matter was not properly justiciable before the courts. For a little over 15 years subsequent decisions upheld this particular aspect of Frankfurter's opinion.[40]

In the Tennessee apportionment cases in 1962 the Court rejected the argument that apportionment was "a political question" and therefore not properly justiciable. This decision has already had and will continue to have far-reaching effects and has been described as the most important decision to be made by the Court since *Brown* v. *Board of Education* and one of the historic decisions of all Court history. *Baker* v. *Carr* was litigated with the United States Department of Justice participating as amicus curiae in favor of court action.[41] In all subsequent apportionment cases the Solicitor General has appeared arguing for more equitable representation in the House of Representatives and in the State legislatures. In short, the Department of Justice has thrown its resources behind those who are working for the principle of "one man, one vote." Whether the decision would have been different without such intervention is difficult to say, but it is simply a fact that the United States, whether as a party or as amicus curiae, has had an enviable record of success before the Court. Particularly noteworthy in this decision is that in other areas of the legislative process generally, the opposite trend has taken place —withdrawal of court jurisdiction over matters clearly within the prerogative of the legislature. For example, the Court has gone very far indeed to establish the principle that the constitutional amending

[40] *Colegrove* v. *Green,* 328 U.S. 549 (1946).
[41] *Baker* v. *Carr,* 369 U.S. 186 (1962).

process is beyond review by the courts. Once the amendments are ratified by the proper number of states and the proper executive official announces and promulgates this ratification, the amendment is adopted. The Court will not question the action of the legislature and executive combined in this function.

The reaction to *Baker* v. *Carr* was, at first at least, surprisingly friendly. More quickly than anyone would have imagined, and apparently more rapidly than the Court expected, cases piled up in higher state courts and lower federal courts. The trend has been to move very rapidly toward greater equalization, and the Court has seemed happy to move along with this pattern. Considering the magnitude of the decision and the warnings of the Frankfurter supporters that "plunging into the political thicket" would create havoc and confusion, the record of judicial reapportionment has been surprisingly successful.

An exception to the generalization that the Court most readily intervenes when there is disagreement between the other two branches is in the field of congressional investigations. The history of Court intervention in this area has been spotty. In response to particular abuses by Congress the Court has intervened in the immediate post-Civil War period, in the 1920s, and again in the last two decades. The Court has generally treated the congressional investigation as a necessary adjunct to the legislative process and therefore as a matter to be trammeled as little as possible. But investigations primarily for informative purposes have always puzzled the courts, for here the investigation approaches a form of nonjudicial trial.

The general proposition that the legislature should and would control its own committees met with few conspicuous disappointments during eras in which the congressional investigation was a relatively infrequent and important tool. But in recent years the tremendous increase in the number of congressional investigations has made the problem more severe. It must be realized that the majority of congressional investigations in all history have taken place within the lifetime of the vast majority of the readers of this volume. As more and more general legislative programs are passed, control of the executive through legislation alone becomes more difficult. There has even been a decline in the importance of legislative control through the budget, as that document becomes more cumbersome, complicated, and unfathomable even to the congressman on the Appropriations Committee.

Congressional investigations provide the means for a quick check on the administrative process. Furthermore, the congressional investigatory committee has become a conspicuous platform for winning popular success, and there have been a number of attempts to use such investigating committees as a vehicle for personal aggrandizement on the parts of individual legislators. When linked with the national security issue and the possibility of continuous investigations of the loyalty of federal employees, however, the investigatory committee looms as a potentially dangerous aspect of the legislative process. The feeling is rife among federal employees and the general public that the Cold War inspired needless investigations that severely damaged the reputations and careers of innocent people and has even contributed a word to the English language, *McCarthyism.*

Responding to this feeling, the Court has in fact intervened directly in an area essential to the life of the Congress. It has done so rather gingerly, generally under the guise of technicalities that were largely, although not completely, remediable by committee action. For example, it has insisted that there be a quorum of the membership of the committee present when any alleged contempt of the committee is said to have taken place in order for prosecution to be possible. It has required that a witness be directly informed of the fact that he is running the risk of being held in contempt. It has insisted that investigations take place with a clear authorization from the Congress for the committee to hold that kind of an investigation. Finally and most broadly, it has insisted that the investigation must be in connection with a valid legislative purpose.

In the latter provision inheres the most likely possibility of a limitation upon the whole investigatory process, for it leaves to the discretion of the Court to decide what is in fact a valid legislative purpose. As of this writing, the Court has not indicated specifically what kind of limitations these would be in practice and how severely Congress would be hampered by the rulings. It would appear, though, that these are so far not major restrictions on the investigatory power and that Congress remains quite free to pursue its own ends.

But it remains of interest that the Court has challenged the Congress on this matter without strong visible support from the executive. It is perhaps not too surprising, therefore, that the majority of the Court that has developed these limitations on the investigatory power has been on the whole the most tenuous shifting of all majorities in any area of constitutional adjudication. This is a question which has sharply divided the Court and caused consternation to its individual members.

In the field of administrative law the Court has carved out for itself an interesting niche, but mostly at the urging of Congress. Until the Court fight of 1937 the tendency of the judiciary had been to resist the advance of administrative power and to substitute their own judgments for pragmatic administration in the name of the "rule of law." After the 1937 struggle the judiciary withdrew almost completely from this field and deferred to the administrative agencies. In one case Justice Jackson even accused the Court of deferring to an expertise the agency admittedly did not have inasmuch as the case was one of first impression.

In 1946, as a result of agitation by the American Bar Association and other groups, the Administrative Procedure Act was passed by Congress which proceeded to judicialize a good many of the operations of the administrative agencies. Among other things the Act adopted as the standard for review of administrative decisions a slightly more imposing requirement. The courts were not to reverse administrative decisions without "substantial evidence on the whole record," as opposed to the former standard which required merely that there be "warrant in the record" to support the administrative decision. While in fact and in logic there is remarkably little difference between the two notions, the courts have interpreted the Administrative Procedure Act as indicating a mood in which greater judicial review of decision would be possible. No great dramatic events have occurred in the past few decades to reverse the tendency toward administrative autarchy; nonetheless, the Court has recouped at least its legal authority to rule on questions before the administrative agencies.

Particularly in areas where an agency has not demonstrated its expertise or competence the Court has shown a tendency to reverse administrative decisions rather more frequently than in former years. All of this has been done under the direction of congressional statute. Whether or not the courts would have moved in the same direction without the congressional hint is difficult to say; at least one authority denies that any such congressional hint was intended. But the fact remains that the Court's effort to control some of the aspects of administration was advanced under the flag of congressional authority.

F. Summary

In the aftermath of 1937 Court fight, Edward Corwin, our greatest constitutional writer, predicted that the Court would re-establish itself as an authority and would in time achieve greatness as the balancing agency between the Congress and the Presidency. That prediction has hardly been vindicated.[42]

The Court has neither retreated timidly nor advanced aggressively in dealing with the other branches of government. In general, the deference to Congress as well as to the states in the field of economic policy is broad. Congress has been upheld in every exercise of its economic powers since 1937, and it is difficult to imagine a circumstance in which the Court would challenge legislation under current standards. There is also strong deference to state action with more frequent Court intervention. Court control in that area is, however, subject to veto or correction by Congress. That is true whether the action proceeds in the nature of statutory interpretation or in the name of constitutional doctrine.

On the other hand, the Court has indicated its desire to remain in business in the American system by intervening in a number of small but vital areas with regard to the exercise of the legislative and executive processes. Although it has conceded certain areas in the domain of the legislature and the executive as completely beyond the bounds of review, these have been nicely and narrowly defined. At the same time, the judges have marked areas in which they will intervene for special reasons. This limitation of Court action to areas where the executive or the legislature would otherwise operate unchecked and in most instances where they have had a history of somewhat irresponsible action enhances the Court's intervention and justifies it. The justices have reacted to a serious challenge and have shown a greater mastery of their political environment.

42 Edward Corwin, book review in **56** *Harvard Law Review* (1942), p. 487.

CHAPTER 5

Role and Doctrine: The Individual and Government

A. An Era of Court Intervention

THE ROOSEVELT COURT and its successors have all been pre-eminently civil liberties courts. Critics assail this simple fact; supporters glory in it. So distinguished a figure as Federal Judge Edward Dumbauld complained that one had to be from among "pickaters, prisoners, proselyters, publicans . . . , and pigmented portions of the population" in order to gain some recognition from the justices.[1] Critics sneered at the bench as well as the particular member when they talked about "justice tempered with Murphy." But the Court has stood behind its espousal of human liberty and has drawn strong support from interest groups and the press as well as the general public.

It was in civil liberties, after all, that, as Robert McCloskey put it, the Supreme Court found a new role.[2] Given the Court's position on economic policy and on the necessity for judicial subordination to the legislature, this role has not been achieved without pain. The call for "judicial self-restraint" has easily been expanded into a call for restraint on questions of civil liberties as well; deference in the one area seems to require deference in the other. The advocates of a civil liberties role for the Court have therefore taken great effort in developing reasons to explain why it is peculiarly appropriate for the Supreme Court to act in this field.

In an era of big government, big labor, and big industry, the protective stand of the Court on civil liberties is most important. The development of procedural niceties as well as broader doctrines for

[1] Edward Dumbauld, "Judicial Review and Popular Sovereignty," **99** *University of Pennsylvania Law Review* (1950), p. 201.

[2] Robert McCloskey, "The Supreme Court Finds a Role," **42** *Virginia Law Review* (1956), p. 735.

protection of individual rights is a necessity not only within the governmental structure but within other organizations as well. The notion of due process that is the heart of procedural protection at the governmental level has led organizations like General Motors and the United Auto Workers to develop courtlike agencies to protect the individual worker and dealer against bureaucratic abuse. Adolph Berle believes that there will be further and more dramatic expansion of these review boards in the industrial complex in the future.[3]

Besides the expansion of bureaucracy throughout our society, external threats also provide the occasion for the denial of traditional individual liberties. But the courts have perceived that there was more than just the defensive need for protection *against* executive excess. They have positively sought to strengthen individual rights with new protection by making it incumbent upon the government to provide adequate affirmative safeguards. Perhaps the most dramatic example of this has been the requirement that where an accused does not have the money to provide a court of appeals with a transcript of his court record, the government has a duty to do so.

The effort to protect the citizen against government effectively involves control by the Court of state action, for the impact upon day-to-day life of most citizens is greater from the regulatory power of state governments than from that of the national government. This "nationalization of the Bill of Rights" has entailed some erosion of state power. Prior to the Civil War the Court had consistently held that a state's conduct toward its own citizenry was largely free from any federal supervision. The leading case is the 1833 decision in *Barron* v. *Baltimore,* where even alleged confiscation of property by a state was held to be outside any federal control.

The Fourteenth Amendment altered the situation by requiring that "no state shall deprive any person of life, liberty, or property without due process of law." While this wording was identical with the similar provision of the Fifth Amendment, it had a subtly different meaning in popular discussion as a result of rather overbroad use of the term *due process of law* by abolitionists and Southerners over the slavery controversy.

There is, therefore, justification for the action of the Court in using the Fourteenth Amendment as a stronger peg on which to base their jurisdiction over the states than they ever attempted to do with the same wording as applied to the federal government. At first the Four-

[3] Adolph Berle, *The Twentieth Century Capitalist Revolution* (New York: Harcourt, 1954).

teenth Amendment was used almost exclusively in connection with economic freedoms—the right to own property, the profit rate, the regulation of prices by state governments, and the access of an individual to the market or employment. From just before the turn of the century until 1937 the due process clause was interpreted as a limitation of the right of the states to interfere with economic freedom as envisioned largely by laissez faire economists.

As to the other civil liberties that we usually associate with the name of freedom—speech, religion, press, and the like—these were not in the early period thought to fall within the ken of the justices. Though some members of the Court wished to extend all of the provisions of the Bill of Rights to the states, the majority resisted and has continued successfully to resist the notion that the due process clause requires enforcement of the Bill of Rights as such against the states. The suggestion that the "liberty" required by the Fourteenth Amendment is identical with the Bill of Rights was pressed by the first Justice Harlan and today by Justice Black; it has been derided as a position that suggests that *liberty* is "shorthand" for the Bill of Rights.

The dominant view on the Court since *Twining* v. *New Jersey* in 1908 [4] has been that "basic" rights under the Bill of Rights may very well be included in the due process notion, but that is because they are "basic" and not because they are in the Bill of Rights. Their presence there may be helpful to the judges in guiding them to what is essential to liberty, but they may find that other nonenumerated rights are essential or that some of the Bill of Rights provisions are not essential. These notions, best expressed by Cardozo in *Palko* v. *Connecticut* [5] and by Frankfurter in many cases, have been derided in their turn most effectively by Justice Black, who has suggested that it constitutes the "accordion theory" of the Fourteenth Amendment. He suggests judges may expand or contract the definition of "liberty with due process" as they see fit.

In fact, however, the justices have not contracted the list of rights by exempting any item once it has been conceded as "basic." The process by which the justices include a liberty as protected under the Fourteenth Amendment is strange and mysterious, but it does seem to be irreversible. On the other hand, a decision that a matter is not covered does not seem to be quite so permanent. Freedom of speech

[4] 211 U.S. 78 (1908).
[5] 302 U.S. 319 (1937).

as against state action was brought under the protection of the federal government in *Gitlow* v. *N. Y.* in 1925, with the somewhat cryptic notation that "for present purposes we may and do assume that freedom of speech and of the press—which are protected by the First Amendment from abridgement by Congress—are among the fundamental personal rights and 'liberties' protected by the due process clause of the Fourteenth Amendment from impairment by the States." [6] The right of assembly was held to be protected by the Fourteenth Amendment only in 1937 and religious freedom in 1940.

Respect for local authority seems to have precluded any major movement by the Court into the supervision of criminal procedure, but small incursions into this area have usually been greeted with popular support, even though generally subject to police criticism. Therefore, little by little, the Court has moved to expand its authority over criminal procedure as well. The earlier stand of the Court in the search and seizure question was that only patently shocking searches and seizures were prohibited to the states, whereas the federal government was prohibited from all "unreasonable" search and seizure. The states, by what has been called a double standard, were free to do many things that the federal government clearly could not allow, and the use of evidence so seized was permitted to the states though denied to the federal government. But this double standard has been eliminated in recent years.

Similarly, the Court has not tried to impose the rigid requirements of the Bill of Rights as to other criminal procedures upon the states in any one sweeping decision. Rather, they have gradually extended the notion of a "fair trial" to cover local proceedings, while slowly but unmistakably increasing the severity of these standards. This process has drawn general support from most sources. Certainly the increased insistence upon the providing of an attorney in criminal cases has been the subject of little controversy. The past few years have seen an extension of the requirement of representation by counsel in criminal trials to aspects of litigation other than the technical trial itself. The Court has extended the right of indigents to be protected in the obtaining of the court record, as we have noted earlier. And while there has been no effort to impose the federal requirements of a jury in criminal cases to the states, there has been an insistence on the equity of the selection of a jury, should there be one.

The nationalization of civil liberties and the assumption by the

[6] *Gitlow* v. *New York,* 268 U.S. 652 (1925), 666.

Supreme Court of the role of protector of the individual citizen even as against his own state government has been effected also under the equal protection clause of the Fourteenth Amendment. Racial discrimination against the Negro has been outlawed in public schools and in public accommodations generally. This has been accompanied by a broader definition—or, more accurately, definitions—of what constitutes state action, and therefore involves the question of whether "public" discrimination is outlawed by the equal protection clause. The rights of Japanese-Americans to own land in California and on the West Coast generally constitute another example of increased Court concern with the liberties of individuals. And while the apportionment cases, as the Solicitor General of the United States himself admitted, reflect a deeply political conflict between the interests of urban and suburban voters against those of rural voters, the Supreme Court's intervention is based primarily upon the equal protection clause and the defense of the individual, wherever he may be located.[7]

B. The Protection of Economic Rights

In the field of economic policy, the Court has moved to diminish its role of authority over the national and state governments, even if the name of individual liberty is invoked. But even in this area there is a tendency to misunderstand the Court's position. While considerations of economic policy are avoided, the justices have insisted upon and expanded the standards for compensation when property is taken. The difference is important, for the Court will not generally stand in the way of governmental action in order to accomplish broad regulatory programs, but it will insist upon justice being done to the individual as a consequence of the policy.

The protection of property has always been one of the major interests of the United States Supreme Court. The Constitution itself was intended to protect property, as Charles Beard pointed out and his critics do not deny.[8] Largely through interpretation of the contract clause of the Constitution, Marshall was able to prevent serious alteration in the vested rights of property owners. On occasion Courts even decided cases in favor of property without invoking a specific

[7] Archibald Cox, "Constitutionalism in Change and Crisis," unpublished address, April 15, 1964, pp. 12–13 (Department of Justice release).

[8] Robert E. Brown, *Charles Beard and the Constitution* (Princeton: Princeton University Press, 1956); Forrest MacDonald, *We The People* (Chicago: University of Chicago Press, 1958).

constitutional provision, relying upon "the spirit of our institutions." [9]

The passage of the Fourteenth Amendment gave the justices a new and stronger vehicle for the protection of property. At first the justices resisted utilizing the Fourteenth Amendent to any major extent just because of the ambiguity of its provisions and the overample scope it provided for judicial intervention. But by the last few years of the nineteenth century the judges became more willing to utilize the Amendment to strike down state economic legislation; as we have noticed, it took 30 years more for them to embrace the protection of civil liberties under the same constitutional provision.

Notions derived from the dominant laissez faire economic and political philosophy of that era became subtly intermixed with constitutional provisions on due process. By the 1920s and 1930s the Court had effectively established the position that wages, hours, and price fixing were virtually outside the scope of state action. Effective rate regulation for utilities was constantly thwarted by continuous · judicial intervention. Particularly when price regulation was involved, the Court was reluctant to allow any action.

Since 1937 the Court position has been quite different. The case that set the new course was *West Coast Hotel* v. *Parrish*. Hughes pointed out for the Court that the Constitution does not speak of freedom of contract, but only of liberty. He suggested that liberty "is thus necessarily subject to the restraints of due process" and "regulation which is reasonable in relation to its subject and is adopted in the interests of the community is due process." [10] By 1941 the Court declared it "too late in the day" to challenge the principle of price regulation.[11] And in 1949 Justice Black explained that the Court had been moving closer and closer to the principle that so long as specific constitutional provisions or definite federal laws were not violated, the states had the power to "regulate what they find to be injurious practices. . . ." [12]

The Court has even sustained programs that are highly dubious from an economic standpoint. Such regulations as Oklahoma's prohibition against the duplication of eyeglass prescriptions from the glass itself rather than through a new eye examination has been upheld. Since 1938 the Court has not used the due process clause to

[9] *Terrett* v. *Taylor*, 9 Cranch 43 (1815).

[10] *West Coast Hotel* v. *Parrish*, 300 U.S. 379 (1937).

[11] *Olsen* v. *Nebraska*, 13 U.S. 236 (1941).

[12] *Lincoln Federal Union* v. *Northwestern Iron and Metal Company*, 335 U.S. 525 (1949), 536.

strike down economic legislation except where there was an assertion of the right to tax property not held physically within the bounds of the states. Here, in at least one sense, the due process clause virtually becomes the same as the commerce clause and an attribute of federalism rather than of property rights.

Simultaneously, the Court also relaxed the restrictions imposed upon the states by the contract clause. They made clear that the states maintain the power to alter their general policies with regard to contracts though they could not single out and change a specific contract. In 1934 Hughes held "the reservation of essential attributes of sovereign power" to be an implied clause in mortgage agreements between individuals. He found this was necessary "as a postulate of the legal order." [13] And in 1945 Frankfurter pointed out that while the public interest may often become enmeshed in a network of private arrangements, the state's authority to protect its people cannot be denied "by abstracting one such arrangement from its public context." [14]

Theoretically, the Court has not abandoned its supervisory role under the Fourteenth Amendment and the contract clause. As Samuel Hendel put it over a decade ago, the decisions "mean simply that the Court is presently disposed to award considerable discretion, short of finality, to a legislative determination of reasonableness and justice divorced from additional hampering restrictions imposed by special doctrine." [15] In fact, however, the tendency of the Court is increasingly to deny review because the decision is a foregone conclusion.

The stand of the justices with regard to the states is identical with their attitude toward the national government. "It is equally immaterial that such state action may run counter to the economic vision either of Adam Smith or of J. Maynard Keynes, or may ultimately be mischievous even from the point of view of avowed state policy." [16] Economic doctrines are irrelevant, as is past practice, as far as the justices are concerned. "As to the argument from history . . ." observed Cardozo, "this would not prove even if no others were then known that the forms then accepted were not subject to enlargement. . . ." [17] In the field of economic policy the justices tread softly,

[13] *Home Building and Loan* v. *Blaisdell,* 290 U.S. 398 (1934), 435.

[14] *East New York Savings Bank* v. *Hahn,* 326 U.S. 230 (1945), 232.

[15] Samuel Hendel, *Charles Evans Hughes and the Supreme Court* (New York: Kings Crown Press, 1951), p. 136.

[16] *Osborn* v. *Ozlin,* 310 U.S. 53 (1940), 62.

[17] *Steward Machine* v. *Davis,* 301 U.S. 548 (1937), 549.

lest they fall victim to "the danger of sliding from the narrow confines of law into the more spacious domain of policy." [18] "The fact that men will differ in opinion as to the adequacy of any particular yardstick of value emphasizes that appropriateness of any one formula is peculiarly a matter for legislative determination." [19]

So strong is the reluctance of the justices to overstep the boundaries of economic policy that they have refused to apply the equal protection clause to state regulation of economic matters even when there is obvious discrimination—for example, in cases involving river pilots where the laws had been so drafted that only the families of currently serving pilots could become apprentices, or in the case of a Michigan barmaids law that made it uneconomic for women to own taverns.

In only one economic area has the Court decided that intervention is desirable and necessary. That is in the question of compensation for taking property. In general, what is a "taking" as a consequence of governmental action can become a very complex and difficult question. So, for example, the Court has been perplexed by the problem of compensation for owners of homes where the creation of an airport results in regular passage overhead by planes, thus diminishing property rights severely. It is hard to generalize in such legal areas because most cases involve highly specialized questions. But it can fairly be said that the post-1937 Court has been quite generous toward suits for compensation, with all members of the Court, liberal and conservative, proving to be "Fifth Amendment capitalists," as it were.

An important aspect of this development is the fact that Congress has shown unmistakably its desire to have such compensation granted to property owners. The expansion of the right to sue the United States, evidenced in the enactment of the Federal Tort Claims Act, by which the United States voluntarily waives its sovereign rights not to be sued in several classes of cases, has encouraged the courts to accept the notion that government too must pay for its wrongs.

C. The Foundation of the Civil Liberties Position

If the judges are to take a back seat in the field of economics, to defer to the legislature and accept the determination of the ballot boxes with regard to, say, minimum wages, why do they not show the same reticence in the area of freedom of speech?

[18] *Phelps Dodge Corp.* v. *NLRB,* 313 U.S. 77 (1941), 194.
[19] *Gelfart* v. *National City Bank,* 313 U.S. 221 (1941), 234.

When the Court in 1931, under the leadership of Hughes, demonstrated zeal in defense of freedom of speech, it relied upon the older language of the defense of property, now transplanted to a new field. So could Justice Roberts write of an abridgment of freedom of speech as an older Court had written about freedom of contract: "The power of a state to abridge freedom of speech in assembly is the exception rather than the rule." [20] But the notion that freedom of speech should be protected by the courts, though resting upon apparent congressional approval and agreement among the justices, still seemed to need a firmer base than sheer enthusiasm. For otherwise, could not this advance of political liberties be as easily read out of constitutional jurisprudence as it had been read in?

The beginnings of a new answer came with Mr. Justice Stone's famous footnote in the Carolene Products Case, where he attempted to base the new trend of the Court in the context of the constitutional document and thus to provide a unified and integrated theory rising above the tone of caprice or even of a purely individual commitment to freedom:

There may be narrower scope for the operation of the presumption of Constitutionality when legislation appears on its face to be within a specific prohibition of the Constitution such as those of the first ten amendments, which are deemed equally specific when held to be embraced within the Fourteenth Amendment. . . . It is unnecessary to consider now whether legislation which restricts those political processes which can ordinarily be expected to bring about repeal of undesirable legislation, is to be subjected to more exacting scrutiny under the general prohibitions of the Fourteenth Amendment than are most other types of legislation. . . .

Nor need we inquire whether similar considerations enter into the review of statutes directed at particular religions . . . or national . . . or racial minorities. . . . Whether prejudice against discrete and insular minorities may be a special condition, which tend seriously to curtail the operation of those political processes ordinarily to be relied upon to protect minorities, and which may call for correspondingly more searching judicial inquiry.[21]

This footnote presents a vivid and interesting justification of a greater role for the Court in civil liberties matters. The ballot box is the remedy for ills that can be cured by voting. The Court, however, must act to preserve the ballot box. There is a greater judicial role, in effect, when for some reason the electoral process is altered or

---

[20] *Herndon* v. *Lowery*, 301 U.S. 24 (1937), 258, echoing *Allgyer* v. *Louisiana*, 165 U.S. 578 (1897).

[21] *U.S.* v. *Carolene Products*, 304 U.S. 144 (1938), 152, n.4.

threatened. The core of the democratic process is the preservation of the exchange of ideas and the appeal to the majority for support. Any artificial restriction of the means of communication or the isolation of a minority from the electoral process are threats to that core of democracy and must be prevented by all means, including the courts. The majority cannot artificially turn itself into a permanent majority by eliminating the right of the minority to attempt to become a majority.

Stone's footnote is a conglomerate, even though its basic idea is a simple one. The first paragraph is actually not even the work of Stone or of his law clerk, Louis Lusky, who also played a major role (perhaps the major role) in the formulation of the Carolene Products footnote. The first paragraph was contributed by Hughes, who wished to tie the assumption of greater authority by the Court in the liberties area to the highly specific provisions of the Bill of Rights. This notion, suggested over a quarter of a century before by Ernst Freund, has one great advantage: it avoids the danger of unlimited judicial control based upon no specific wording in the Constitution. The notion that the Court ought to stick to the words of the Constitution and to enforce them literally has been accepted as part of his platform by Justice Black.

The second paragraph presents the heart of the Carolene concept —that political freedom, the untrammeled exercise of the democratic process, is uniquely the province of the judiciary to defend, even against majority action. In one sense, all dominant theories on the right of free speech today accept this notion; in another sense, it is the basis of the division among the various schools. While all agree that the free exchange of ideas is to be protected by the courts, the question is, to what extent should the courts be the primary or chief defenders of the process? What weight should the Court give to a legislative action which the judges might feel abridges freedom of speech?

The "judicial restraint" wing of the Court, led by Justices Frankfurter and Jackson, urged that while legislation affecting free speech should be viewed with "a jealous eye," the Court must on the whole "balance the interests" in this area as well as in other constitutional areas. This device tended to settle the question against individual freedom, however; the judicial balancing generally took place between the diminution of freedom for any one person and the alleged threat or possible threat to national security threatened by nullification of the congressional statute or federal or executive program involved.

Almost invariably, the "interest balancers" found for the government and not for the individual.

The period of the 1940s saw a conflict between those who, like Frankfurter, wished to identify the role of the Court in civil liberties pretty much with its role in economic matters, and a less unified school identified with Stone's central notion, the "preferred freedoms" approach, maintaining that laws involving abridgment of freedom of speech were not just to be looked at with that jealous eye but were to be scrutinized with hostility, perhaps presumed to be unconstitutional.

The preferred freedoms approach had rather bad luck. First of all, its proponents could not agree on exactly what they meant by the phrase, and this was obvious from the beginning. Secondly, a whole series of peculiar circumstances resulted from the fact that there was never a single opinion in which the preferred freedoms doctrine was accepted by a majority of the court. For example, in the Carolene Products Case four justices acquiesced, but Justice Black, who later became one of the preferred freedoms leaders, did not agree with the section of Stone's opinion in which the footnote appeared. Then too, Justice Frankfurter attacked it with all the force of pen and logic he could command. Finally, just when it seemed that the Court might move to accept this doctrine, death removed from the Court Justices Rutledge and Murphy, the most emphatic of the libertarians.

As the Cold War grew more frigid (or hotter, if you will), the preferred freedoms wing of the Court began to lose strength. Now, sometimes in lone dissent, Justices Black and Douglas moved to a more extreme, somewhat veiled, position. Justice Black in particular began to accept the notions of Alexander Meiklejohn, philosopher and former president of Amherst College, who had argued that the First Amendment was an absolute defense of freedom of speech. Going beyond the central notion of Stone's Carolene Products footnote, Meiklejohn argued that there could be no limitation whatsoever exercised upon political freedom. The thinking process of the community could never be mutilated under any circumstances, and no censorship or other wartime condition could constitute the basis for denying any genuine intellectual and political position whatsoever. To deal with the problem of slander and threat and profanity, Meiklejohn suggested that there were different kinds of speech. Only public speech, related to the market place of ideas, was protected by the First Amendment. Other types of speech were encompassed by the Fifth Amendment, and there denial of liberty could take place as long as there was no violation of the concept of due process of law.[22]

Black was cautious in embracing this absolute position on free speech, perhaps as a consequence of the preferred freedoms fiasco, perhaps because he was genuinely troubled and unsure of his ground. It was only through the writings of his former law clerk, John P. Frank, that he made a preliminary statement, in the early 1950s, of his acceptance of the notion of absolute freedom for ideas.[23] And it was not until 1960, in a lecture at New York University Law School, that the Justice himself openly stated his position. The following year, in an interview with Professor Edmond Cahn of the same law school, Justice Black delivered a much greater bombshell. In an interchange with Professor Cahn he revealed that he had come to the conclusion that slander and libel laws were in fact impediments to free speech prohibited by the First Amendment. He had arrived at an absolutism greater than that of Meiklejohn—an absolute absolutism, so to speak.[24] Government may prohibit actions; words may be evidences of illegal action, but the words themselves and the ideas themselves cannot be prohibited.

Black's stand is certainly the most advanced ever taken by any American judge of his repute. Even before this revelation, Charles Black of the Yale Law School (no relation to the justice) had suggested that Justice Black was following a conscious tactic of constantly raising the ante—taking a more extreme position than likely to be accepted—with regard to the protection of the citizen's right of free speech.[25] If this is the case, then Black's strategy was brilliantly conceived. He kept alive the notion of judicial protection during a period in which he and Justice Douglas were often its only spokesmen. Since that time, although Warren and Brennan and Goldberg have established a more activist majority and the most effective spokesmen for an opposing viewpoint have left the Court, Black has continued to stay one or two steps ahead of the Court.

[22] Alexander Meiklejohn, *Free Speech and Its Relations to Self Government* (New York: Harper, 1948); reissued as *Political Freedom* (New York: Harper, 1960).

[23] John P. Frank, "Review and Basic Liberties" in Edmond Cahn, ed., *Supreme Court and Supreme Law* (Bloomington: Indiana University Press, 1954), pp. 109–139.

[24] Hugo Black, "The Bill of Rights and the Federal Government," in Edmond Cahn, ed., *The Great Rights* (New York: Macmillan, 1963); and "Justice Black and First Amendment Absolutes: A Public Interview," **37** *New York University Law Review* (1962), pp. 569–83.

[25] Charles Black, "Mr. Justice Black, the Supreme Court and the Bill of Rights," *Harper's Magazine* (February 1961), pp. 63–68.

D. The Fruits of the Free Speech Position

Decisions have already been made which move substantially toward the Black position. In 1959 in *Barr* v. *Mateo* the Court made clear (what had probably been accepted as law even earlier) the principle that a government official may not be sued for damages for public comments made in the course of his official duties. More significantly, in the New York Times Case in 1964 the Court made that "absolute privilege" symmetrical: the opinion by Justice Brennan established that criticism of a public official for his official conduct was also privileged.[26]

The decline of the balancing of interests wing of the Court has also been accompanied by loss of prestige for the Holmes formula of "clear and present danger." Holmes had held, largely in dissent, that the government might act to restrain liberty if a clear and present danger of some substantive evil was presented to the legislature. Both of these elements had to be present. The formula proved quite ambiguous when issues of national security arose. Both wings of the Court claimed to speak in Holmes's name, although most commentators seem to agree that Judge Hand and Justice Vinson had seriously altered the formula in the Dennis Case. In that decision, which upheld the conviction of top-rung Communist leaders for conspiracy to organize to advocate the overthrow of the government of the United States, the government alleged a clear danger but was unable to establish a present (immediate) danger. In effect, the Communist leaders were accused of organizing an instrumentality which would at a future unspecified but predictable time advocate the overthow of the government.[27] Writing for the Federal Court of Appeals, Learned Hand—a judge whose reputation was certainly not less than that of most members of the Supreme Court during his lifetime—argued that one must take into account not only the clearness and immediacy of the danger but also the extent of the threat if the danger should develop. A very serious danger did not have to be as "present" as a minor one. The threat here was of the most momentous, the overthrow of the government itself. Therefore, by his formula, "the seriousness of the evil discounted by its improbability," the government was well within its rights in prohibiting the act involved. To

[26] *Barr* v. *Mateo*, 360 U.S. 564 (1959), and *New York Times* v. *Sullivan*, 32 L.W. 4184 (1964).
[27] *Dennis* v. *U.S.*, 341 U.S. 494 (1951).

have instituted the same limitation against freedom of speech in order to avert, say, a traffic jam would be unthinkable, but in view of the threat to the organized society—which was, after all, the basis and the matrix of all free speech—some suppression was legitimate. This suggestion by Hand was adopted by Chief Justice Vinson in his opinion for the majority. Though both maintained that they were following the Holmes approach, most observers agree that they had departed from it and dubbed the variation the "clear and probable danger" test.

The formula did not appeal to the justices in retrospect, for the same argument could be utilized in connection with any idea that implied some "threat" to society, no matter how obscure. The immensity of the threat posed—that is, that somehow free speech would destroy the entire society—could easily be made to outweigh any improbability of its occurrence. So, in *Yates* v. *California* in 1957, dealing with the conviction of second-rank Communist leaders, Justice Harlan went out of his way to emphasize that the Dennis decision did not suggest one could be convicted for mere affiliation with a group that might possibly advocate the doctrine of overthrow. Not only did he rule that the organization of the Communist party had been accomplished in 1946 (and, therefore, that the conspiracy element, always a tricky legal question, could no longer be utilized against Communist defendants); he also made clear that the advocacy involved had to be real, active, individual advocacy and not merely abstract avowal of doctrines. Communist leaders could be convicted for advocating the desirability of the overthrow of the United States government, but only if they did so in a meaningful and committed way. Ideas were not to be outlawed, only actions.[28]

This decision largely fixed the course of subsequent legal doctrine on free speech. Perhaps the most notable thing about it is that it avoids the whole question of clear and present danger. Similarly, there is virtually no mention of any of the other formulas that we have talked about, and such has been the case in many subsequent decisions in the area of free speech. It is almost as if the justices have deliberately agreed among themselves that the use of the older slogans of the 1940s and 1950s contributed little to the discussion of the practical cases before the Court and instead alarmed the public and created an impression of fundamental disagreement among the justices. It may very well be that Justice Black's action in making his declaration

[28] *Yates* v. *U.S.*, 354 U.S. 298 (1957).

on libel off the Court is also part of a general pattern in which cases on free speech are decided pragmatically in an effort to avoid deeper philosophic antagonisms that will make the Court's task more difficult.

We have here discussed free speech cases involving the national government as if the Court assumes the right to dictate to Congress much as it did in the economic sphere in the 1930s. The Court does maintain that it has such power, just as it maintains that it has this power vis-à-vis the states, here indeed on firmer textual and historical grounds. But it is significant that to date there has never been an instance in which a law of Congress was declared unconstitutional as a violation of the First Amendment. All of the cases that we have been discussing involve statutory interpretation—that is, the construction of the law passed by Congress in order to *avoid* a constitutional question. Wherever the Court feels that it may avoid the constitutional question by reinterpretation, it does so. This power, of course, can be utilized in effect to rewrite a statute. To a large extent the Court can accomplish what it wishes to by interpretation, knowing that the forces in Congress are usually so well balanced and the claims on congressional attentions so great that corrective laws are unlikely to be enacted. The Court's role in the field of free speech is different from its modern stance on the commerce clause because in the latter case the Court acknowledges that Congress has the last word; in the former case, even if Congress should act, the Court has ultimate constitutional authority.

In one significant area the Court has without equivocation shown that it regards itself as the prime protector of the individual, and that is on the question of freedom of association. There have been two strong and severe tests of the law of freedom of association in the past three decades. The first instance dealt with the problem of the Cold War and Communist subversion. The second arose from the efforts of some Southern states, in the aftermath of the school desegregation decision, to hamper civil rights organizations and particularly to prevent solicitation of cases to desegregate within their borders. The resultant controversies led to decisions in which the right of association became one of the recognized First Amendment freedoms in regard to both the national government and the states. It was held that membership lists do not have to be made public under conditions that will allow members to be harassed by state action. The Court in a number of ways limited the authority of the national government to prohibit membership by its employees in certain organizations or to require its employees to swear they do not belong to these organizations without procedures protecting the rights both of the individuals and of the organizations. It must be observed that in both instances there are also decisions which have clearly established national and state authority to regulate private associations. By and large, the internal security program of the United States has been upheld in about half of the decisions before the Court. Some of the regulations of the Southern states have also been accepted as valid—subject to review for discriminatory practice—if they are not obviously aimed merely at civil rights organizations.

E. "Separate and Insular Minorities": Apportionment, Religious Freedom, and Desegregation

The third facet of Stone's Carolene Products footnote remains to be explored. It is at one and the same time the most interesting and the most perplexing of the Stone theories. The suggestion is that statutes aimed at particular religious, national, or racial minorities may "be a special condition" which, though nominally not involved in the political process, does in fact curtail the potential influence of these groups so that they are unable to carry their case successfully to the ballot box.

But how does one define an insular minority? Are stockbrokers an insular minority? In one sense every nonmajority is a minority and might be entitled to special protection from the courts. There is some help from the specific provisions of the Constitution—for example, the observation that no religious tests shall be given for office, or the prohibition against discrimination in the right to vote on the basis of sex or race. But the connotations of these provisions are much more limited than the notions in Stone's footnote. In essence, the attitude toward racial and other minorities that currently prevails in our courts is based upon historical experience, a few long-standing precedents, and a strong sense of justice. Stone's argument that the courts are uniquely qualified to protect such minorities may very well be true, but it remains a somewhat queasy constitutional base for this important role.

The major vehicle for the implementation of the minority protection argument of Stone has been the equal protection requirement of the Fourteenth Amendment, prohibiting the states from establishing unreasonable categories in dealing with their citizens. Again, the problem of what is an improper category comes to the fore. Obviously, it is not the mere establishment of categories that is prohibited, for every law in effect establishes categories. The tax law decides who shall pay and who shall not under what circumstances; the traffic law decides that people who have the right of way may continue and those coming along the side street must stop.

Here the courts have a relatively clear-cut and logical answer. A law denies equal protection if the basis of the categorization is irrelevant to the purpose of the legislation for which the category is established. So, for example, I.Q.'s would be a legitimate basis for differentiation in admission to an educational institution, while height and weight would be irrelevant. On the other hand, a state could establish categories based on height and weight with regard to crossing a bridge. It is the contribution of the Korematsu Case that *racial* categories are presumed to be a denial of equal protection and are suspect in American law.

The Court has scrupulously avoided the finding that categories based on economics are arbitrary or unsuited to the purpose of legislation. Just as in the due process clause, the Court has separated "civil liberties" from "economic protection" and has ignored the equal protection clause for most economic purposes. Rather, it has upheld those categories and has left their definition solely to the legislatures. At the same time, it has struck down important barriers to equality on the basis of race, religion, or sex.

The major decision in this field was the reversal of *Plessy* v. *Ferguson* in 1954.[29] Had there been no precedent, it would have been easy to decide that racial categories were not relevant to education, and presumably the Court did decide just that by its reversal. But the earlier decision had been based upon the notion that a system of racially separate schools did not constitute categorization of any type and was simply a matter of convenience; any categorization was for the purpose of maintaining peace in the community and therefore arose not from educational needs but from safety needs. It assumed that such separation as existed in the community was real and reflected true social conditions, rather than being created by law. In this sense *Plessy* v. *Ferguson* was based in the profoundest sense upon a sociological theory of the separation of races.

The decision in *Brown* v. *Board of Education* [30] rejected the claim that separate facilities could be equal. Inasmuch as they were in-

---

[29] *Plessy* v. *Ferguson*, 163 U.S. 537 (1896).
[30] *Brown* v. *Board of Education*, 347 U.S. 483 (1954).

herently unequal and branded the minority group as inferior, there could be no equal protection afforded individuals under these circumstances. The case was based on legal reasoning and precedent along the lines argued here, citing cases that had laid the groundwork for the overthrow of the Plessy decision, cases going back at least as far as 1917, when it had been held that residential areas could not be segregated without creating inferiority. However, in one substantial footnote the Court cited a number of psychological and sociological studies as evidence that separate facilities in education were inherently unequal. It is this footnote, over which commentators have disagreed as to its influence in the final outcome, that Southerners have attacked as proving that the decision was based not upon law but upon fragile behavioral studies of doubtful validity.

Subsequent decisions have repeated this invalidation of racial categories with regard to public facilities generally. For example, in a case that went to the Supreme Court a Negro woman was upheld in her insistence that she be referred to as "Miss Hamilton" rather than "Mary" in legal proceedings, since to refer to Negroes by their first names as though they were servants was a vestige of segregation and branded them as inherently unequal.[31] As the Court has demonstrated in its follow-up to such decisions as *Smith* v. *Allwright* outlawing the white primary, once a decision is reached invalidating a practice, far-reaching efforts to evade the decision will be treated with little lenience by the Court.

A major problem in the implementation of the equal protection clause is the role of the state. Constitutions limit governments, they rarely touch individuals. Certainly this is true with regard to the creation of discriminatory categories; the Fourteenth Amendment clearly applies only to state action. But what is state action? The limits here are rather extensive or very narrow, depending on your point of view. It is relatively obvious that the actions of a paid administrative official pursuant to a law passed by the legislature and promulgated by the governor constitute state action. But would, say, the actions of an official of a party organization in connection with a primary be considered state action? On the one hand, there is the danger of including all activities that have even remote connections with government; on the other, there is the simple fact that without a broad definition of some kind a state could accomplish any discriminatory policy it wished by simply delegating the offending action to a

[31] *Hamilton* v. *Alabama*, 32 L.W. 3340 (1964).

functionary who received his income from fees or contributions instead of the state payroll.

The Court has moved to a liberal definition of state action without encompassing all of the areas it has been urged to include. It was relatively easy to consider the actions of state officials in connection with a primary election as state action, for here the nexus is so vital and obvious as to constitute a real problem under the Fifteenth Amendment, at least as far as the white primary is concerned. Where the state has in effect delegated a governmental power to an agency and has made it a "chosen instrument," the Court finds no difficulty in holding that the Fourteenth Amendment standards apply to the delegated authority. Similarly, where a nominally private organization has really become governmental in scope, there is relatively little difficulty. For example, a company town, although nominally a private organization, has all the attributes of a governmental structure and must therefore assume its responsibilities. But what if private discrimination is merely enforced through the machinery of government? This has presented grave problems, since in fact a good many forms of discrimination are deeply imbedded in our social practices. Some of them we do not label discrimination at all, but merely private choice or caprice. The attitude of the Court can best be described, although in a facile and somewhat misleading fashion, as holding that individual action or isolated practices may be implemented even through governmental structures, but when the practice reaches the proportions of a widespread social pattern, the implementation of the practice by the government and its officials really amounts to a form of legislation. This formula is not without difficulties, and the Courts have had considerable problems in trying to draw the line between merely individual action, however arbitrary, and denial of equal protection of the law forbidden by the Fourteenth Amendment.

The leading authority is clearly the restrictive covenant decision, *Shelley* v. *Kraemer*. The pattern of residential segregation, still the heart of the controversy with regard to education of Negroes, particularly in the North, came into question in that case.[32] A pattern had developed by which a number of landowners would mutually agree that they would not sell to various groups, particularly Negroes. These covenants were voluntary in the sense that landowners did not have to enter into the arrangement, but they were enforceable in

[32] *Shelley* v. *Kraemer*, 334 U.S. 1 (1948).

the courts. In a major effort to end the residential ghettos of the major urban areas, civil rights groups focused attention on this pattern, arguing that it violated the Fourteenth Amendment. Since court enforcement was in fact the very heart of the pattern, they argued that it was forbidden by the equal protection clause. The decision by Chief Justice Vinson held that while such arrangements were not illegal, they could not be enforced by the courts. Individual owners were free to do as they wished, but there was no way in which the machinery of government could be invoked to force compliance with the original agreement. The contracts were not void, but voidable at the discretion of any party. In the Jaybird Association Case, and in some of the recent "sit-in" cases, the Court has gone further in speaking of the prohibition by the equal protection clause of discriminatory social practices having the force of law and enforced by governmental officials. So the existence of a preprimary primary, a caucus agreed to by the governmental officials involved, constitutes part of the election pattern and governmental structure and is subject to the requirements of the Fourteenth Amendment. Trespass can be dealt with by local officials, but an order to "move on" based upon segregation, given by a policeman who knows full well that such a social custom exists, might well constitute state action.[33]

The domain of state action under the Fourteenth Amendment has not been rigidly defined by the Court. In view of the sweeping social changes that are being sought, this is perhaps not too surprising. At the same time, it does open up the Court to criticism even by its defenders.[34]

But it is simply a fact that legal doctrine, especially the more malleable constitutional variety, grows with the occasion as well as the intent. Perhaps the most striking development with regard to the notions of state action is the recent insistence upon the more positive aspects of state conduct. In the Prince Edward Case the plaintiff successfully argued the point that if public education was offered in any part of the state of Virginia, it had to be offered throughout the state. In one sense this represented no great novelty, for the argument of the plaintiffs was that the closing of the schools in Prince Edward County in answer to a court order to desegregate was an evasion of the court mandate and an improper classification. The fact that the courts had ordered desegregation could not be accepted

[33] *Terry* v. *Adams*, 345 U.S. 461 (1953).
[34] For a trenchant criticism see Herbert Wechsler *Principles, Politics and Fundamental Law* (Cambridge: Harvard University Press, 1961).

as an educationally based differentiation.[35] Lurking behind the decision is the further notion that in this day and age it may be that the Fourteenth Amendment requires that all states provide public education, an argument which so far has not been pressed too vigorously on the national level and therefore has not had to be ruled upon.

The apportionment situation presents much the same sort of picture, a gradual evolvement of a definition of strict equality in voting. *Baker* v. *Carr* merely decided that the courts could intervene; subsequently it was decided that within the same district voters had to be counted equally. There could be no such thing as an "equitable classification" or weighted voting within the same district. In subsequent cases the Court moved to establish the principle that substantial equality must be achieved and that there is no classification that permits even the drawing of boundaries on any other basis but something approximating "one man, one vote." All districts for both houses of state legislatures must be substantially equalized, with no weight permitted to area or special accommodation given to any specific interest.[36]

It is important to note that in both the racial cases and the apportionment cases very broad social questions are being adjudicated before the Court. This is unusual but not completely novel. Courts have dealt with problems approaching the magnitude of the apportionment case, but probably never has there been a Court-induced program of the magnitude of desegregation. In both instances the legal question has not been only equal protection of the laws; the actual treatment of the case has been on equitable grounds. Equity, a system of law that developed in England in rivalry to the common law, is more flexible and allows more discretion to the judge. It grew up because of a desire to avoid some of the strictures of the common law system, which sometimes penalized the very people it was supposed to defend. In American law the two have been combined in most courts, though the judges may wear either the hat of equity or the hat of the common law, shifting between the two at times. A quick distinction is to suggest that in the common law people are assessed damages for wrongs already committed, while in equity wrongs are sought to be avoided. If the tearing down of a house would destroy the value of a house built against it, the common law would assay

---

[35] *Griffin* v. *County School Board*, 322 F. 2d 332 (1963).

[36] *Baker* v. *Carr*, 369 U.S. 186 (1962); *Gray* v. *Sanders*, 372 U.S. 368 (1963); *Westberry* v. *Sanders*, 32 L.W. 4142 (1964); *Reynolds* v. *Sims*, 32 L.W. 4497 (1964).

damages after the second house fell down because its supporting wall had been removed. In equity an injunction could be sought against the destruction of the first house.

In the apportionment and segregation cases the equitable considerations involved gave the Court vast discretion in drawing up its remedy. So the peculiar pattern of district enforcement of *Brown* v. *Board of Education* accepts the wisdom of adaptation to local circumstances. In the apportionment case *Colegrove* v. *Green* the crucial vote of Justice Rutledge was based upon his opinion that no equitable purpose would be served at that time by attempting to eliminate unequal districts.[37]

While the segregation decision was the most far-reaching in terms of actual social change, the apportionment decision may ultimately have even greater legal consequence. That stand is fully consistent with the proposition that the Court is the unique protector of the political process and the supervisor of the heart of that process, free access to and use of the ballot box. The Court decision moves us further toward a majoritarian and egalitarian society and makes the Court role more anomalous. Judicial review, Corwin once wrote, is American democracy's effort to cover its bet. Now it becomes the bulwark and indeed the architect of majoritarian control. Only time will tell whether the democratic spirit so aroused will eventually eliminate judicial review or will honor the Court that fostered it, enabling the judicial prestige so engendered to be utilized elsewhere, on other issues.

F. The Individual as Citizen and Civilian

A relatively uncharted area of American jurisprudence, until recently, is the domain of the rights of citizenship. Shrouded in confusion and controversy, the original provisions of the Constitution on citizenship were directly involved in the very origin of the Civil War. A major purpose of the Fourteenth Amendment was to reverse the Dred Scott decision and to provide a more definite notion of what American citizenship entailed. As usual, the provision put to rest some of the previous controversies, only to create new ones. The pre-eminence of national citizenship is now evident in the first clause of the Fourteenth Amendment. And the grounds for acquisition of citizenship are equally plain, birth in the United States under the

[37] *Colegrove* v. *Green*, 328 U.S. 549 (1946).

authority of the government of the United States being sufficient for citizenship, regardless of any other attributes of the individual. This was settled in the Wong Kim Ark Case, which decided that citizenship on the basis of geography and not on the basis of blood was the law of the United States so far as any person born within its borders was concerned.[38]

All persons born or naturalized in the United States are citizens; in addition, Congress confers upon children of American nationals the status of citizenship even if they are born abroad. Thus we have supplemented *Jus Soli,* law of the place, with *Jus Sanguinus,* law of blood or kinship, for our residents abroad. While this presents interesting conundrums, such as the question of whether Franklin D. Roosevelt Jr. (born in Canada of American parentage) or George Romney (born in Mexico) are "native-born Americans" and therefore eligible for the Presidency, these are side issues. A much more fundamental question is the nature of the other end of the process, when and how one gives up American citizenship.

In international law any government defines its own citizenship. Some countries have tried to hold on to their citizens regardless of their personal wishes and regardless of the passage of time. It was once the custom of the Japanese empire to claim that the descendants of any citizen were Japanese citizens regardless of the number of generations that had intervened. Swiss citizenship is so conferred, and in recent years Jacobo Arbenz, deposed as President of Guatemala, was able to get a ruling from the Swiss government that he was in fact by descent a Swiss citizen.

American citizenship has never been this unremitting. We have generally felt that an individual should have the right to relinquish the privilege of citizenship if he wishes. And there are further reasons for establishing criteria regarding when an individual gives up American citizenship, for it has been the custom of a number of individuals to maintain multiple citizenship and to manipulate these to their advantage. Thus, they can claim American citizenship when they wish protection, while claiming perhaps Panamanian citizenship with regard to taxation. Congress therefore specified that taking an oath of allegiance or fulfilling functions in the government or military service of another country is incompatible with loyalty here and constitutes the relinquishment of American citizenship. Similarly, Congress at-

[38] *U.S. v. Wong Kim Ark,* 169 U.S. 649 (1948).

tempted to make evasion of the draft and flight from the country under specified conditions indication of an intent to deny citizenship. Finally, Congress established many conditions under which a naturalized citizen might lose his citizenship, including renewed residence for a number of years in his native country or simply extended residence abroad. In a series of decisions the Court has proceeded to strike down, perhaps to the vanishing point, the disabilities set by Congress upon naturalized citizens and to protect all citizens from inference of intended renunciation of citizenship.[39]

In questions of citizenship the Court has in recent years not only reasserted its intent to declare congressional measures unconstitutional; it has acted to defend the individual in an area where the consequences to him are very great. No other agency but the Court can intervene once Congress has passed a general statute. The statement of the Court that denial of citizenship can constitute "cruel and unusual punishment" is perhaps an understatement in a world of passports and red tape. Identity is so firmly linked to citizenship that it is almost paralyzing to think of the individual without such a national affiliation.

Similarly, the question of identity of the citizen arises in a very dramatic way at the borderline of the division between the civil and the military. Just as the problems of citizenship have become much worse in a world of antagonisms, so, of course, the "garrison state" situation of the Cold War has exacerbated the problems of civil versus military dominance. Again, the Court has chosen to defend the civilian sector. It has demanded that civilians be tried by civilian courts, re-echoing a stand as old as the Reconstruction period. For example, when the military attempted to recall reservists into active duty for the sole purpose of trying a civilian in a military court, the justices balked. The Court has also attempted to draw sharp lines between the civil and the military by denying the right of military courts to try civilian dependents abroad. Even when these intrusions of military law have had the tacit support of Congress or where, as in the case of crimes long since committed or committed in service abroad, there is no other vindicator of law available but the military, the Court has clung to the principle of civilian autonomy. This insistence that the civil sector be as protected from military control as is possible under modern conditions of war is a vital contribution to the protec-

[39] *Schneider* v. *Rusk,* 84 S.Ct. 1187 (1964); *Kennedy* v. *Mendoza-Martinez,* 372 U.S. 144 (1963).

tion of the individual in our society. The exact line of division could not always be drawn, but the principle that there is some such a demarcation is a necessary bulwark of American democracy.[40]

Even more adventurously, the Court has attempted to limit the effects of internal security programs. In an era in which the government is the major industrial contractor of the nation, industrial security programs affecting civilians can for all practical purposes become police scrutiny programs for all workers in our society. The justices could not but be aware of the importance of espionage in modern war or of their own incapacities to evaluate in any detail the extent or the dangers of espionage. Courts are not good agencies for specifying security regulations. But they have been effective in rectifying gross injustices to specific individuals or in finding specific security programs so overzealous as to be unjustifiable. It is still politically a matter of judgment and controversy whether they have hampered American security. It does seem fair to say that no evidence has been adduced that the Court has in fact caused major dislocations to the security program.[41]

G. The Individual and Religious Liberty

The proper domain of religious liberty remains one of those central problems facing all societies and inadequately solved by them throughout history. Stone's Carolene Products footnote assumes the propriety of the defense of religious minorities without further justification; neither does it explore the limits of that protection. Such fundamental problems as respect for individual conscience—with regard not only to military service but also objections to taxes, inoculation of children, use of harmful drugs or practices which might endanger the individuals involved if embedded in religious belief present special dilemmas. Rights of the majority with regard to religious freedom are as hard to reconcile and satisfy as the needs of minorities.

American society has generally taken a pragmatic view toward its religious problems. So, for example, we exempt from military service

[40] *Toth* v. *Quarles,* 350 U.S. 11 (1955); *Reid* v. *Covert,* 354 U.S. 1 (1957).
[41] *Peters* v. *Hobby,* 349 U.S. 331 (1951); and *Cole* v. *Young,* 351 U.S. 536 (1956). In an interesting example of how such legal principles are generalized and gain support from groups nominally not affected in the original cases, principles of these cases have recently been applied to supporters of General Walker who had been dismissed for activities apparently contrary to military regulations.

conscientious objectors who believe it violates their religious conscience to bear arms. We allow adult Jehovah's Witnesses to refuse blood transfusions but remove children of such Witnesses who might die without the transfusion from the authority of their parents and appoint temporary guardians who permit the transfusion. We insist that pacifistic religious groups pay taxes, but we attach property in order to obtain the sums rather than throw the protestors in jail, since they believe that payment of money to a government constitutes a tribute to Moloch.

This type of gentle pragmatism was violated in the first Flag Salute Case in 1940 when Justice Frankfurter held for the Court that the children of Jehovah's Witnesses could be forced to salute the flag. The outcry over this decision was such that several members of the Court recanted and in an identical case held that school children could not be compelled to salute the flag. Indeed, Justice Jackson held that there was no need for the children to even assert the claim of religious liberty; nothing could force them to salute the flag for any reason, and any exemption they chose was justifiable. Subsequent rulings on a lower court level have held that the pledge of allegiance with its wording "one nation under God" presents no dilemma for atheists, since under the flag salute decision they may omit the words with impunity.[42]

But not all problems lend themselves to such nice solutions. What of religious instruction and prayers in the schools? It is obvious that the Court has a role here, for the First Amendment specifies that Congress shall pass no law "affecting an establishment of religion," and under any of the theories of the Carolene Products footnote the Court is obliged to intervene when there is a specific constitutional provision on the matter. Furthermore, it has been held that religious freedom is one of the fundamental rights encompassed by the Fourteenth Amendment and therefore subject to court control as against the states as well. While the justices have spoken of a "wall of separation" between church and state, the line has in fact been a wavering one.

With regard to religious instruction as part of the educational process the Court has wavered. In their initial decision the justices held that religious education may not take place on school grounds. Only four years later the Court seemed to retreat, for it limited its holding in the McCollum Case to one set of facts: if the children were

[42] *West Virginia* v. *Barnette,* 319 U.S. 624 (1943).

released from the school in order to take instruction, the program was constitutional. The fact that the coercive machinery of the school was utilized in the New York system was not held to be relevant. (Though no sums of state money were involved, regular truancy provisions were invoked, and if a child did not attend religious instruction he had to return to regular classes.) [43]

In one area the justices have been firm. They have maintained that prayers may not be said in the schools, for this constitutes a form of worship. Further, the reading of the Bible as a devotional exercise constitutes a form of religious practice. These decisions have been as controversial as any in the history of the Court. And while official governmental resistance is not being loudly announced—there are some exceptions, as in Alabama, where the Governor threatened to pray in the schoolhouse door—there is probably no area where there is more actual violation of Court decisions than with regard to the place of religion in our educational system. [44]

All of this does not mean that the Court will strike down any law alleged to be in violation of the consciences of a religious group. The Court sustained the law prohibiting the Mormon practice of polygamy in Utah. While some pluralist theorists such as Harold Laski have argued that this constitutes a grave violation of religious freedom, there seems no movement on foot even within the official Mormon Church to revive that custom. Snake worshippers may not freely handle poisonous snakes with impunity. Christian Scientists may not prevent others from studying physical hygiene in the schools, though they themselves may be exempt from any requirement. And it is argued by such thoughtful and libertarian spokesmen as Dean Griswold of the Harvard Law School that by analogy prayers ought to be allowed in the schools as well. This will not exacerbate relations between various groups in our society, argues Dean Griswold, and it might well engender respect. Where better might the different religious groups in our society learn to accommodate and to understand each other's religious traditions?

Defenders of the Court's attitude on prayers tend to give this a rather brusque answer. It is not education that is forbidden but worship; it is not social harmony that is at stake but the constitutional separation of the domain of Caesar and God. As the late President Kennedy pointed out rather succinctly, there are other places to pray

[43] *Zorach* v. *Clauson,* 343 U.S. 306 (1952).

[44] F. Sorauf, "Separation of Church and State," in C. H. Pritchett and Alan Westin, *The Third Branch of Government* (New York: Harcourt Brace, 1963).

besides the schools and better ways to worship than under coercion.

The dilemma of the Court in maintaining religious freedom is nowhere better exemplified than in the series of cases involving Sunday closing laws.[45] The origin of these laws was clearly religious, yet they were also sustained by a notion of economic and social well-being based upon leisure. The facts of competitive economic life made it desirable that a closing day be established by law rather than by personal convenience. But what of the individual whose religious conscience forced him to close on some other day of the week? Presumably he was already obtaining sufficient leisure, and yet he must be closed on Sunday as well. Yet the problems of the state in policing the day of rest might require that everyone take the same day off. The Court accepted the contention of the states that what was involved was an economic policy and did not permit exceptions because of religious preference, on the grounds that such exceptions might be inconvenient to supervise and that it was within the discretion of the state legislatures to decide on the desirability of such exemptions. The effect is to place an economic liability upon such groups as Orthodox Jews and Seventh-Day Adventists, but many economic regulations put burdens upon classes of individuals without creating problems of discrimination.

Perhaps the Court's decision was matter of strategy; at a time when it had challenged the basis of prayers in the schools and the segregation question and was to embark upon the apportionment question, it might have been wise to avoid further entanglement when the laws of the state could be restated in terms of economic regulation. Yet, at about the same time, the Court had no difficulty in invalidating a requirement of the state of Maryland that prospective officeholders declare their belief in God. It would appear that even in the field of civil rights the Court is much more inclined to act where legislation affects individual conscience rather than where a social policy is involved. But there can be no better example than the Sunday closing laws to uphold the proposition that the Court by and large sustains economic regulation in the name of the state while it acts to defend civil liberties against the state.

[45] *McGowan* v. *Maryland*, 366 U.S. 420 (1961), and companion cases.

CHAPTER 6

Compliance

A. The Problem of Compliance

PERHAPS NO single word, not even *certiorari,* is currently heard so frequently in the halls of the Department of Justice and in legal circles generally as the word *compliance.* On one week end in April 1964 the Attorney General, the Deputy Attorney General, and the Solicitor General all gave major public addresses attempting to analyze and promote support for compliance with Court decisions. This interest is reflected in scholarly studies of the Supreme Court as well.

Constitutional interpretation tends to emphasize different intellectual problems in different eras, reflecting the needs of the day. At the turn of the century theorists were preoccupied with the question of legitimacy of judicial review—was Marshall justified in his decision in *Marbury* v. *Madison?* The 1920s and 1930s witnessed discussions on the possibility of reconciling majority rule with judicial control, a more sophisticated and still unsettled problem. In the 1940s and early 1950s discussion centered on the meaning of the Supreme Court fight of 1937 and the general role of the Court in our political system. Since *Brown* v. *Board of Education* (1954) there has developed a new appreciation of the limits of Court authority to effect social change. This inquiry brings into focus legal effectiveness as well as legal limits, as both are part of a single relationship, and for the full picture both must be understood.

It is easy to see that Court decisions are only at first glance the end product of the judicial process. If they are not enforced, clearly their meaning is nullified. "I can call spirits from the vasty deep." "Why so can I, or so can any man, but will they come when you do call for them?" [1] Andrew Jackson is alleged to have said it more plainly: "John Marshall has made his decision, now let him enforce it." All of law requires cooperative actions; imagine income tax enforcement if each and every taxpayer rebelled at each possible stage of the process.

---

[1] William Shakespeare, *Henry IV,* Part I, Act III, Scene I.

The vision of nine, black-robed "old men" trying to compel the U. S. Army to give up control of the steel mills throughout the United States is perhaps an amusing one. But the most important fact about the Youngstown case is that President Truman and his administrators accepted the decision without question. On the other hand, studies have shown persistent violation of Court rulings now 15 or more years old on religious instruction in the public schools. Integration decisions, though not ineffectual, have at the same time hardly secured full compliance either.

It is, of course, the integration situation that has dramatized and called attention to the intricacies and limitations of the Court's power through the actions of the lower courts and state legislatures to thwart or delay Supreme Court policies. Then too, the situation has demonstrated the reliance upon federal and above all local officers for enforcement of ordinary Court decisions, and therefore the inherent possibilities for neglect, opposition, or alteration in policies as they filter down the line. Finally, it has clearly shown that the ultimate acceptance or nonacceptance of a decision lies in the behavior patterns of the "recipients" or "consumers" of the policy, who may be, as in the segregation cases, virtually coterminous with the general public itself, or may involve a dozen or so highly specialized and well-publicized individuals such as stockbrokers. But it must be borne in mind that while the integration crisis has alerted the public to the general problem of compliance, it has not been the sole focus of attention. It has led to a general inquiry that has illuminated the problem of enforcement generally. Compliance is not only a central problem in the understanding of the social order but a major problem of statesmanship and creativity for the members of the Court itself.

B. Sources of Resistance

Following Barnard and Simon, we may say that in any policy hierarchy general statements of intent are transmitted downward and are intended to be obeyed.[2] Subordinates accept and obey such statements—assuming first they can understand the message—for a variety of reasons. They may implement the policy because they agree with it or reap advantage from it. On the other hand, even if they have reasons to oppose the policy, they may be moved to support it

[2] For an authoritative statement which also exposes the welfare economics basis of the approach, see James March and Herbert Simon, *Organizations* (New York: Wiley, 1958), pp. 84–90.

because of practical considerations, including the costs of opposition. Finally, there may be such unquestioning respect for the authority transmitting the policy that costs will not be calculated. Barnard labeled the area of acceptance without consideration of advantages and disadvantages the "zone of indifference."

We can therefore distinguish several areas of possible motivations for compliance—personal utilities, organizational utilities, and psychological utilities—and can create a matrix of possibilities of combinations of advantages and disadvantages. Obviously compliance is at its greatest when personal advantages are highest, organizational sanctions against opposition are certain and severe, and the legitimacy of the issuing authority is acknowledged. Conversely, it will be at its minimum when the individual utilities all point in the direction of opposition, organizational sanctions are lenient and—most important—erratic in application, and the legitimacy of the higher authority is doubtful. The difficulty is in the ordering of the possibilities in the intermediate areas. For example, in the absence of sure punishment there is considerable evidence that severity is often—perhaps always—irrelevant. The classic example is the gangs of pickpockets that used to infest the crowds assembled to witness the hanging of unsuccessful pickpockets in England. No one knows how many units of legitimacy compensate for how many units of other utilities, for what kinds of persons under what conditions. In general these happen to be the interesting questions.

The effort to apply this approach to the Court implies an additional problem. In the transmittal of policy American Courts follow prescribed channels that make it most difficult for the higher court to follow up on enunciated policy. Cases come up normally in their own good time; the higher courts have few opportunities to state their program regularly and periodically, even should they seize every chance. Lower courts have considerable option in dealing with the interpretation of decisions. In any event, the implementation of higher authority is a difficult art, and judges can expect to be reversed. Indeed legal circles do not accord any prestige to judges with extremely low reversal rates, for they regard this as indicating a lack of creativity and imagination on the part of the judge. At his discretion a judge may ignore precedent, distinguish the case from older rulings, or find new conditions to differentiate a particular case from previous ones.

State courts in particular may find grounds in state law for disposing of a Supreme Court ruling and therefore inferentially or even directly stating the irrelevance of the federal position. So, for example, the Florida State Supreme Court attempted to prevent integration of its University of Florida Law School on grounds that preservation of the peace, a local concern, was the real issue and that integration was quite irrelevant.[3] Or the lower court may accept the general findings of the precedent and recognize the policy to the extent of giving one side a moral victory, but by limiting the practical implications of the decision grant in effect the actual victory to the other side. Whether or not the higher court can then effect its will regardless of the lower court depends upon the timing of subsequent cases on the same question and the intensity of feeling in the higher court. If cases develop at a pace commensurate with that of the flow of events the upper court may in fact be effective. But this requires a determination to devote attention to cases of a certain type at the expense of attention to other kinds of questions.

John P. Frank has considered this in a discussion of the "practicalities of power." Here he points out that the Court has been hampered in effecting its patent policies because the matter is not normally sufficiently pressing in any one instance to justify the Court's occupying itself in continuous review of administrative and lower court findings. Patent administrators have refused to respond to cues from the Court to raise their standards for originality in the granting of patents. Of course, they do comply in specific cases to avoid defying the Court directly, but they have made no move to change their general policy. An active Court concerned with more pressing problems than the Patent Office has necessarily conceded the *de facto* power of the agency to pursue its own course; the Court simply cannot give this question sufficient priority to force its own will. Reliance upon legitimacy and psychological factors of authority here having proven inadequate, the Court has not chosen to exercise its authority to intensify the effects of the sanctions involved and increase the costs of defiance.[4]

On the other hand, in segregation matters the Supreme Court uses all the major devices it has at its disposal to control the lower courts. Summary reversals, anticipatory statements of intent concerning fu-

[3] *Florida Ex. Rel. Hawkins* v. *Board of Control,* 390 U.S. 413 (1956) and 351 U.S. 839 (1956). An unusual demonstration of Supreme Court authority came in *U.S.* v. *District Court* 371 U.S. 18 (1962), when the Court ordered a district judge to obey its ruling, via mandamus if necessary. No one in the Justice Department could recall a comparable situation.

[4] John P. Frank, *The Marble Palace* (New York: Knopf, 1958), pp. 24–41.

ture cases, and detailed directions for enforcement have all been utilized to make the Court's integration policy clear and emphatic. By placing great importance upon the unanimity of decisions and the degree to which the Court is committed, by emphasizing the intensity and high priority of their commitment and the certainty of sanctions against transgressors, the Court has clearly sought to induce compliance.

In general, the obstructionist potential in legal matters, as we have seen with regard to the patent office, becomes greater when general policy is involved than when the ruling concerns a specific matter. This is true not only with regard to lower courts and administrative officials but also with regard to the conduct of private individuals. A characteristic of Court policymaking is that it is not typically addressed to particular individuals outside of a very small and relatively insignificant number of cases. Rather, it is a generalized, full-blown discussion for guidance to all who might come within its purview. The form of decision belies realities; in spite of the appearance of the judicial decision as being an answer to the question at hand, the real importance of a decision lies in its policy applications.

Paradoxically, opinions are generally of such length and ambiguity that expert reading and exegesis is nearly always necessary to find out who should be reading the case. Courts establish rights for "all the world"; they seldom know in what place or time what kinds of individuals will eventually be affected by their decisions. Like legislators, judges come and go, but their precedents live on. And while legislative action has the force of policy only until its is repealed, even overruled precedents live on in Court annals. When laws are passed, they are generally designed to meet specific situations, though ambiguities of intent often lessen the vigor of their application. Legal decisions are designed for universal application, and judges are therefore inaugurating a radiating policy with each decision, and sometimes even, as we have noted, with every sentence that they write. Statutes affecting specific types of individuals can usually be found in a short time under a limited number of headings. Legal decisions that might affect a class of persons are almost unlimited in scope inasmuch as legal principles can bob in and out of cases on any subject. Judges therefore must face the expectation that precedents will not always be known to lower courts or, even more important, to administrators.

The crucial function of the legal profession in compliance is evident. The lawyer, "the one indispensable adviser" in our modern society, is the single major conveyor of legal policy to its ultimate consumers. One may take as an example an entire area of law such as libel and slander, where it is quite safe to suggest that all the legislation and decisions have virtually no effect on the day-to-day behavior of the average citizen. Effectively, the law of libel and slander is simply a check on the mass media through their daily contact with attorneys. Similarly, the law of parental liability is unknown to the general public, which enforces a stricter accountability than do the courts.

The bar in its interpretative role may encourage or deter opposition to the law. By undertaking or refusing to undertake litigation lawyers may challenge, alter, or develop the implications of a doctrine. Continuous litigation allows a higher court both to clarify and to enforce its will. Current Southern efforts to brand NAACP litigation as illegal and the social pressures in the South that have kept the numbers of civil rights lawyers to a minimum are highly effective deterrents to compliance. Without lawyers there are no cases; without cases there is little opportunity to expand old doctrine or create new ones. The enforcement process becomes more difficult when lawyers' actions are paralyzed.

C. The Court and the Presidency

The dependence of the Court on executive enforcement in extreme cases of defiance is historically and logically so self-evident that the justices themselves openly discussed it long before the segregation cases drove this point home in recurring executive interventions in Little Rock, Alabama, and Mississippi. Military intervention is the ultimate sanction, to be avoided when at all possible. Executive enforcement through the activities of the Department of Justice radiates down to the level of local district attorneys. In addition, orders to operating departments to facilitate or discourage compliance as well as the use of the governmental contract and purchasing powers as leverage to secure compliance are all at the disposal of the President. It is equally within the President's reach to thwart a Court decision, although the conflict he would create for his subordinates is a clear deterrent to any such action of defiance. Inasmuch as the President himself must bargain, exhort, and trade to maintain effective executive leadership, he treads on dangerous ground if he encourages the flouting of authority.

The President also plays a major role in popular compliance. His public pronouncements have great importance in dramatizing the issue and encouraging support or resistance. His words are an earnest of future conduct. Eisenhower's refusal to indicate approval of the segregation decisions and his indications that he "could not conceive" of circumstances that would impel him to utilize troops are generally felt to have precipitated a situation testing just that disposition. Andrew Jackson's toast, "The federal union, it must and shall be preserved," on the other hand, was well understood as a commitment and helped to avoid the use of force. In recent years President Kennedy's mild defense of the prayer decision compared to President Johnson's official neutrality may well have had important effects.

Presidents rely so much upon legitimization as a vehicle for their control of subordinates that they cannot afford to defy the Court. A refusal by Truman to obey the steel seizure decision would have been as revolutionary a step as would a military move to take over civilian government—both physically feasible propositions, at least in the short run, and yet unthinkable in the current context of American society. Both remain outside the "zone of indifference" in the minds of any set of administrators currently in a position to carry out such measures.

The political impact of traditional respect for constitutional equilibrium was well illustrated in the celebrated Court fight of 1937. President Roosevelt had just been elected by an overwhelming majority. Yet his proposal aroused strong opposition among his own supporters and led to his defeat on the measure. What he suggested —the appointment of an additional justice if an incumbent chose to remain on the Court after reaching 65—was clearly within the letter of the Constitution and amply precedented. Only one aspect of Roosevelt's plan, to break up the Court into smaller panels to expedite cases if the total number of justices became too large, was of doubtful constitutionality. But the opposition felt that the package as a whole was unacceptable and that it would be wrong to upset the balance between the various agencies of government. Nonetheless, the provocation in the 1930s was extreme. The Court was dangerously out of step with the depression-born demands of the country and had been the focus of controversy for decades. Still, an overwhelmingly popular President could not gain his way in changing the Court, let alone in challenging it as an institution.

The story might have been different if the justices had not reversed their objectionable constitutional rulings. The results of the Court fight of 1937 have been admirably epitomized by the saying that

Roosevelt the politician got a legal victory while Hughes the Chief Justice won the political struggle. The Court and its power remained intact, but through the "switch in time that saved nine," restrictive constitutional limits on federal power were altered and swept away.

Robert Dahl's formulation of the relationship between the Court and the other branches of government seems most accurate—i.e., the President alone will not normally bring the Court to heel, but President and Congress together can.[5] In the long run a majority in control of both the Presidency and the Congress is dominant. In the short run the President alone has great weight but must, within the clearly recognized sphere of the Court, generally follow its lead.

D. Congress and the Court

While foreigners are perplexed by the extent of Court powers, Americans are rather surprised by its limits. The whip hand of Congress particularly, though based upon powers quite familiar to constitutional authorities, is unknown to the average citizen. Charles Curtis has labeled the Court a "tenant at sufferance," whose power is subject to direct congressional control.[6] While the dependence of the Court upon the Presidency, though real, is indirect and pragmatic, its dependence upon congressional approval is direct and formal.

Since the Court does not determine the number of justices, Congress could, with presidential approval or over his veto, increase the number of sitting justices. (Whether they could force a President to make appointments or seat someone pending an appointment seems doubtful, however.) By increasing the number, they could, with the President's help, directly alter the tenor of the Court's decisions. It was, after all, the power of the Prime Minister to flood the British House of Lords that forced that body twice in this century to acquiesce in a curtailment of its own powers. The same weapon could be used in America, although since 1937 it might be argued that altering the composition of the Court has acquired an anticonstitutional tinge.

Less sensational but hardly less potent is congressional authority over the appellate jurisdiction of the Court. Congress is enabled to make "exceptions" and "regulations" to the appellate jurisdiction of

---

[5] Robert Dahl, "Decision Making in a Democracy: The Supreme Court as a National Policy-Maker," **6** *Journal of Public Law* (1958), pp. 279–95.

[6] Charles Curtis, *Lions Under the Throne* (Boston: Houghton Mifflin, 1954), p. 35.

the Court and could thereby exclude from consideration by the justices any subject on which Court and Congress were in disagreement. Bills already exist which define Court jurisdiction on the basis of the amount of money involved, when the case was filed, the type of court having original jurisdiction, and the nature of the parties as well as the subject matter of the litigation. It is apparent that exceptional ingenuity is not necessary in drawing up a statute excluding a matter from Court consideration. After all, even due process of law under constitutional protection does not require that every type of case must eventually be adjudicated in the Supreme Court of the United States itself so long as a fair legal hearing process is observed somewhere along the line.

Constitutionally, the congressional power seems unlimited. Henry Hart, Jr., has argued that Congress could not so deprive the Court of authority that it loses its status as a "supreme court." [7] Small exceptions to its jurisdiction hardly seem to threaten that standing, however. Even a large number of exclusions would still leave the Supreme Court as the highest of all legal authorities. When Congressman Howard Smith of Virginia sought in 1958 to end the power of the Court to declare that a state law had been by implication superseded by an act of Congress—a proposal defeated by one vote in the Senate—Joseph Rauh, Jr., of the Americans for Democratic Action argued that it was "anticonstitutional" if not unconstitutional, threatening the fabric of American liberty.[8]

But on the whole, the difficulties with such exclusions are more practical than constitutional. In the first place, the Court has shown great skill at least in administrative law in permitting review where Congress had seemed to forbid it. More important is the possibility of lack of uniformity that will result if state courts have the final word on interpretation of their own statues and on the question of whether their laws comply with federal standards. A "subversive" bill might have a commerce clause effect and might not be reviewable if the state supreme court so decided. Final decision at the court of appeals level in federal questions is hardly more satisfactory, the potential for conflicting interpretations of federal law in different

[7] Henry Hart, Jr., "The Power of Congress to Limit the Jurisdiction of Federal Courts: An Exercise in Dialectic," **66** *Harvard Law Review* (1953), pp. 1,362–1,402.

[8] Testimony of Joseph Rauh, Jr., "Limitation of Appellate Jurisdiction of the United States Supreme Court," Committee Print, Senate Judiciary Committee, 85th Congress, Second Session, p. 45.

parts of the country being rather obvious. In truth, Congress has faced the fact that making exceptions to the Supreme Court's jurisdiction is a doubtful remedy with sure side effects, and has sought other, more satisfactory alternatives.

Surprising as it may seem, many Court decisions can be altered by the Congress. Constitutional amendments are possible. Often too, Congress can use its powers to let a decision stand as law while reversing the total effect of the decision. If Congress wishes to alter a decision that was favorable to government property rights, it is rather simple to appropriate the sum or the property involved to the individuals whose claims have been denied. For over a century Congress has regularly done just this.

Other powers of Congress can, of course, also be utilized to change the law for future parties, particularly if it is a question of statutory construction in the first place. Since 1937 the Court has after all developed as its key role in the interpretation of the will of Congress. Alan Westin speaks of this as the emergence of Congress as a "higher court of revision" over the Supreme Court itself. In the most thorough search undertaken so far Westin found no less than 50 occasions between 1944 and 1960 where Congress had so acted, with 34 efforts successfully overturning some 60 Supreme Court decisions. Further, these included highly significant actions such as the Tidelands Oil Case and the portal-to-portal pay program. All but three of the "reversals" dealt with economic matters. In view of the continuous controversy over the civil liberties decisions of the Court, this fact suggests a strong vindication of the Court's political judgment.

Further, Westin points out that characteristically Congress acts directly and self-consciously to rebuke the Court for the error of its ways. The enacting clause for such legislation typically recites the wrongdoings and misconceptions of the justices and indicates that the Congress now reluctantly but firmly sets matters right. The standard charge of "judicial legislation" that congressmen levy in conjunction with such matters is perhaps a consequence of congressional uneasiness at their own new role of "legislative adjudication." As Westin points out, the typical subject matter for such remedial legislation is broad in scope and even "semiconstitutional." [9]

Just how common this has become was illustrated when Congressman Emanuel Celler of New York, the Democratic Chairman of the

[9] Alan Westin, "Corporate Appeals to Congress for Relief from Supreme Court Rulings," unpublished paper, American Political Science Association, September 1962.

House Judiciary Committee, proposed a substitute for a constitutional amendment on prayer. He suggested a resolution indicating that the intent of Congress was that voluntary prayers should be considered constitutional. (Clearly such a resolution has no real authority, and Congressman Celler, a supporter of the Court decisions in this area, may well have been engaged in a diversionary tactic.) Even more remarkable was Senator Dirksen's 1964 proposal to postpone the implications of the apportionment decision by a rider to a foreign aid bill. The use of such standard legislative maneuvers rather than more formal separate legislation indicates the growing familiarity with which Congress reverses the Court.

No study has been undertaken to estimate the number of Court decisions heavily criticized in Congress, but these would surely constitute a small fraction of the total number. Most never come to the attention of Congress at all. Court standards are, however, frequently utilized in discussions in the halls of Congress as tests for prospective legislation. Such standards are an important factor in the drafting and passage of legislation. The possibility of its being declared unconstitutional is, of course, an important weakness in any bill. Additionally, Court standards are relied upon as symbolic weapons even in instances where there is little or no likelihood of a case ever developing in the area. The question of constitutionality is raised and discussed independently of Court decision in American politics as well. A public statement that a law is unconstitutional may mean that one predicts its invalidation by the Supreme Court, but it can also have the more British meaning of simply expressing strong disapproval based upon some sense of the proper dimensions of government. It is therefore not only possible but quite usual for congressional debates to include appeals to constitutional principles that are essentially personal values. A truly effective argument in this vein is usually based upon actual Court decisions, and congressmen love to dwell upon cases and exhibit their legal prowess. This positive use of past decisions is a significant aspect of Court influence over the legislative process. In spite of the headlines over their opposition, the normal reaction of Congress and congressmen toward the Court is one of compliance and respect.

In a very real sense the functions of Congress and Court overlap. Wallace Mendelson and John P. Roche have advanced the theory that the Court is most active when other governmental agencies are paralyzed as a consequence of the failures of party discipline. Stuart Nagel has examined several possible meanings of this theory and rejected them, but on rather slim grounds.[10] Conversely, Westin points to the action of Congress when "business" joins the coalition of anti-Court forces to rebuke and reverse the Court. While this is a strictly contemporary—and rather vague—explanation of operating forces, it, like those previously mentioned, may serve to stimulate further analysis.

E. The Court and Local Governments

A major purpose of the Constitution was to transfer authority over individuals to the federal government in order to allow the direct exertion of federal authority in vindication of its own actions without reliance upon the states. But the states do in fact exist, and their authority survives. Severe problems arise when state authority is asserted in counterpoise to federal action or when individuals clothed with local authority put themselves in opposition to the national government. Because the states under the federal system retain a rudimentary sovereignty, their officials can stage a virtual civil war.

The problem of convincing a state to comply is one that admits of no easy solution. The Supreme Court, which has had nearly two centuries of experience with such cases, uses all its ingenuity to avoid the problem. Under its original jurisdiction, for example, the Court hears suits between states. These have been typically long drawn out affairs. In the celebrated case of *Virginia* v. *West Virginia,* decades passed before final resolution of the matter. The Court frankly treats such cases more as matters of arbitration than as questions of law, encouraging the states to settle the matter themselves if at all practicable.

In the face of determined state opposition to a decision the Court has followed the same tactics of delay. Rather than risk an affront to their moral authority, the justices have usually accepted half a loaf or even a gesture, assuming that time would produce acquiescence or at least diminish the intensity of opposition. In stressing the continuity of its moral authority even at the risk of foregoing a victory the Court follows the pattern of other institutions like the Catholic Church, which instills respect through its moral standing rather than through the imposition of sanctions. The Court, like the Church, has

---

[10] Wallace Mendelson, "Judicial Review and Party Politics," **12** *Vanderbilt Law Review* (1959), pp. 447–57, and Stuart Nagel, "Political Parties and Judicial Review in American History," *Journal of Public Law* (1963), pp. 328–40.

not sought to challenge and test the limits of its power, preferring to display the impression of power.

States' assertion of their right to make constitutional interpretations is perhaps older than the Court's own official claims. The Virginia and Kentucky Resolutions, personally inspired by Jefferson, stopped a trifle short of an open claim but did make clear the Jeffersonian argument that constitutional interpretation was a joint product of many agencies with no final or determinant authority. Congressional remission of fines levied under the Alien and Sedition Acts (1798) was an early example of the possibilities of congressional reversal of Court decisions and was later cited by Justice Holmes as tantamount to an admission that the Acts were unconstitutional.

Jacksonian reassertion of national power undercut the interposition doctrine—on which, in fact, most states had never taken a stand. Yet almost simultaneously the Court found it necessary to retreat in a number of cases involving state grants of land and state authority over Indians. During the abolitionist period as well the Court handled a whole series of challenges on the fugitive slave laws, and in 1861 the justices held that the constitutional provision that a governor must return escaped prisoners on request of another state was the statement of a moral rather than a legal obligation, thus obviating the need for Court intervention when a governor refused.[11]

But not all such showdowns could be averted. Since then the Court has made it clear that open challenges to federal prerogatives will be met. Typically though, action is undertaken at the weakest point of state power, mainly through moves against subordinates rather than, say, against the governor or the state government as an entity. Moving against the most vulnerable members of the bureaucracy is an immensely effective method; it thrusts the local official into a dilemma he can best solve by obedience to the federal authority, since the Constitution directly binds him to vindicate national law, "anything in the laws or constitution of the states notwithstanding."

The Court has made clear its right to consider the actions of a state in realistic terms and to delve beneath the state's or the governor's interpretation of what events actually are. This is so even over such matters as public safety. In a leading case in 1932, for example, Chief Justice Hughes held that a governor could not proclaim an emergency requiring extraordinary executive prerogatives and that the Supreme Court has the right to ascertain independently whether

[11] *Kentucky* v. *Dennison,* 24 Howard 66 (1861).

such conditions exist.[12] Similarly, in the segregation cases the Courts have reluctantly moved in response to direct defiance by governors. It is not too much to say that in the Mississippi cases Governors Barnett and Johnson were found guilty of contempt because they themselves insisted upon such a verdict.

In general it is organized local opinion, having the backing and force of law, that presents problems of compliance for the Court. The tradition of compliance is so forceful that counterjustification must be formally created to sustain disobedience. As Alexander Leighton has written, "Human groups cannot effectively carry out acts for which they have no underlying systems of belief." [13] In order to develop this sense of countercommunity, a spokesman must emerge. The most obvious and natural such center of opposition is the executive of state or local government. His compliance or disobedience often determines whether there will be local compliance. As operative head of a government with police powers, and as a legislative leader in his own right, the American governor can precipitate situations that threaten compliance. As leader of a commonwealth he has the stature in his own community which approaches that of the President in the national community.

Because of the legal form in which Court decisions are cast, and because he is the state's chief legal officer, the state attorney general often becomes involved in state-Court disputes. His responsibilities and practical powers are many; it has been estimated that two thirds of the administrative law of a state like Ohio is the handiwork of the attorney general. In doubtful cases his rulings may speed up compliance, with desegregation as in West Virginia or Delaware, or he may provide legal props for opposition, as in Georgia.

But opposition can equally focus around a local officer like the colorful and powerful Judge Perez of Plaquemines Parish, or a school board, or even a justice of the peace. Public office is just one of many fulcrums for leadership that can be utilized to implement opposition or compliance.

In general, state office is most likely to become the focus for opposition to Supreme Court rulings. There is a tradition, a lingering legitimacy to state defiance. The structure of American federalism encourages state officers to speak jealously of their prerogatives and national encroachment in a way not yet standard for local officials.

[12] *Sterling* v. *Constantine,* 287 U.S. 378 (1932).
[13] Alexander Leighton, *The Governing of Men* (Princeton: Princeton University Press, 1945), p. 292.

State complaints about national authority are part of the normal griping of American politics, something like mother-in-law jokes, perhaps reflecting certain aspects of reality but not often meant seriously or taken as fact. Yet, these repeated invocations make the states a natural rallying point against national authority.

Once a state, or any other unit, has breathed defiance, it will usually find continuous opposition easier to accept in other cases. It has redefined its zone of indifference; it has consciously devalued the legitimacy of obedience. It is not surprising that Governor Wallace of Alabama, bowing only to overt federal compulsion over desegregation, should also come to oppose the prayer decision, for he no longer automatically accepts Supreme Court decisions as legitimate without further examination.

Southern forces have provided the motive force in attacking the Court on other grounds in addition to desegregation. They have chosen what they regard as the Court's most vulnerable points. First declaring their own dissatisfactions through such broadsides as the Southern Manifesto—signed by virtually every Southern congressman —they have encouraged criticism of the federal courts for alleged lack of concern for internal security, overindulgence in legal niceties on the protection of persons accused of crime, and general usurpation of authority in such matters as apportionment. At one time their efforts cast a wide net and drew strong and diverse support, but the coalition fell apart and now seems wrecked beyond repair.

At least one writer, C. Herman Pritchett, has suggested that the anti-Court coalition was doomed precisely because of its segregationist base,[14] but actually it was destroyed by the changing trend of world events and by its own unfortunate choice of issues. As the international situation grew more complex, presenting a challenge to creative statesmanship, a mixed strategy of decisive actions based upon less fixed positions undercut the "Fortress America" notion of tight-lipped security. The Court's protection of the accused criminal continued to tap the well of American sympathy, arousing unsuspected reservoirs of idealism even within the American bar. Even the controversy over control of congressional investigations did not prove a good issue for rallying the anti-Court forces, for there was already an almost universal feeling that Congress had been—and is still— badly remiss in not achieving better substantive and procedural con-

[14] C. Herman Pritchett, *Congress Versus the Supreme Court* (Minneapolis: University of Minnesota Press, 1961), p. 120.

trol of investigations, a feeling shared even by many who did not want to see the Court take a hand in the matter.

More recently efforts have been made to attack the Court on the issues raised by *Baker* v. *Carr* and the prayer decision. But the reapportionment issue splits Southern forces more decisively than it gains Northern adherence for any anti-Court movement. Conservative, Southern, suburbanite Republicans, normally a major force in the anti-Court fight, are precisely the most adversely affected group under gerrymandering and the one that can benefit most from reapportionment.

Even the prayer issue, potent as is its appeal, seems to have created its own backlash. On sober second thought many of the groups thought to have favored a pro-prayer amendment seem to have emerged in the opposition camp or to have developed strong doubts. The California congressman who was the original sponsor of the prayer amendment and who later withdrew his support is a good example of this trend.

In short, the Court has accurately interpreted its own strength relative to that of the political forces facing it. But its decisions clearly entail risks. Time Magazine has quoted an anonymous observer: "The Court is either brave or stupid, and does not appear stupid." [15]

Of course, the Court has initial advantages that help to conceal errors of judgment, that shield it for a time from the consequences of any growing antagonism. The inertial effects of public respect for the institution, fear of change, and the support of groups dependent upon the Court all have to be overcome in order to produce opposition. In turn, criticism must become strong enough and exhibit enough staying power to overcome the various fences that have been built to preserve the balance of powers in American politics. The problem of pushing Court reform legislation through Congress, in Senator Clark's phrase the "sapless branch" of American government, the graveyard of many a reformist or counter-reformist movement, is particularly vital.

Insulated from immediate consequences, the Court in the past blindly continued to arouse vocal opposition that characteristically took a decade or two to stir up politically effective consequences. Often preliminary skirmishes preceded the ultimate rebuke. Some present-day commentators are concerned that the path of the present

[15] *Time Magazine,* May 22, 1964.

Court may lead in the same direction. At no point in history, they argue, has the Court attempted to control more aspects of governmental life in more far-reaching ways than in the past decade. Such attempts, they say, belong in the category of Hughes's "self-inflicted wounds"—steps toward bitter conflict if not institutional suicide. Supporters claim, however, that the Court's powers are enhanced if not ennobled by intelligent and creative use of its authority. Only time will tell which position is correct.

Opposition is organized most effectively not on a national level but on a state level, through state control over such things as the licensing of meetings and parades, corporate law, the relationship between organization members and attorneys, and the like. The state governments, after all, are the initial, and in our day the major, determinants of the proper scope of free discussion—what is said—and also of the mode of all discussion—when and under what conditions it is said. Having the primary and major burden of protecting discussion—the whole requirement of maintenance of public order—local authorities must exercise control as well. Refusal to permit meetings and close enforcement of other requirements can be an effective tool in the mounting or silencing of reaction to the Court.

On the positive side, state officials, particularly in the Southern states, have attempted to develop their own point of view through state machinery, particularly the so-called state sovereignty commissions. These function as publicity agents and rallying forces for segregation. The Virginia commission, for example, has issued a number of impressive documents designed to advance the Southern cause. In Mississippi and in other states the commissions are authorized to defend actions commenced against individuals in much the same way that the Attorney General of the United States is authorized to act under the 1964 Civil Rights Act. Transfer of litigation and its attendant expenses from an individual to the state is, of course, an important encouragement for defiance, as it eliminates a major deterrent, the fear of court costs.

In sum, the local authorities emerge as focal points for resistance where there is possible conflict, but, of course, they are equally the keys to the achievement of compliance. In a number of instances firm support of desegregation by local officials inspired compliance where such a result had not been anticipated. So, South Carolina moved with little trouble, though under duress, while Virginia reflected the sense of turmoil of Governor Almond's capitulation made with a bitter denunciation and put up further resistance.

Yet it would be an error to assume that leadership has always been the primary element. In many instances it has been clearly the case of the officials shouting like Carlyle's French Revolutionary figure, "The mob is in the streets. I am their leader. I must follow them." In Alabama, Governor Folsom was repudiated as a moderate, Senator Lester Hill received the scare of his long political career, and Representative Albert Rains retired rather than risk the defeat experienced by Carl Elliot. Similarly, in Louisiana the Long dynasty, which had avoided identification with anti-Negro forces for three decades, was backed into a corner to the point that Russell Long emerged as one of the "sparkplugs of the civil rights filibuster." On the other hand, segregationist leaders like "Bull" Conner of Birmingham and the pro-Faubus school board at Little Rock have been repudiated by the voters. When the community stand is solid, regardless of the intensity so long as the attitude is relatively universal, the community leaders can ratify the implicit consensus or establish it in a context that is unchallengeable. This is especially true of the school prayer cases. On this issue community sentiment is usually relatively fixed, particularly in homogeneous rural areas. Boards of education commonly ignore Court rulings forbidding religious education in the schools. While some districts did move into compliance, school boards and superintendents generally persist in following their own views or the unstated reactions of the community.

Resistance thus has many components besides leadership. It may be localized or distributed throughout the country. Further, some issues are characterized by resistance at the core of the intended target of a policy, as in segregation, while in other issues the decision is accepted but enforced only against the most conspicuous violations, as in apportionment. It is not improbable that most successful social control measures follow the latter pattern, with the fringe violations corrected or ignored at the discretion of the local community. So, for example, the persistent violations of the prayer decisions in rural areas of homogeneous religious faith obscures the potential of these rulings for the urban setting, where the problem is most acute.

F. The Court and Public Opinion

The torrent of public criticism and billboards calling for the impeachment of Earl Warren notwithstanding, compliance with routine decisions of the Court can be taken for granted. Otherwise, of course, the whole legal order of which the Court is the apex would be endangered. Even in controversial issues the moral force of Court approval is usually a positive one. When the Court ruled that Jehovah's Witnesses could be compelled to salute the flag, anti-Witness riots broke out in scattered parts of the country with mobs shouting, "The Supreme Court is with us." Use of the segregation decision in moral discourse by civil rights groups is common and was climaxed by a ten-year anniversary celebration to mobilize public opinion and raise funds.

In view of the Court's dependence upon general public respect, it is anomalous that the public seems to know very little about the Court. A 1945 poll showed only that two fifths of the adults questioned even knew the number of Supreme Court justices; assuredly, only a miniscule number of that group fathom legal intricacies.[16] Public opinion tends to veer between bland admiration of the justices when no issues are raised and cynical oversimplification of the judicial role when decisions are made which do not accord with particular interests. Efforts to convey more realistic appraisals of the Court do not seem to have penetrated deeply; in fact, they have actually exposed the Court to more devastating criticism.

The problem of conveying to the public what the Court does has absorbed commentators, professors, and the justices themselves for some time. The legal technicalities, the modes of procedure, and the self-imposed limits on propriety in discussing their own work all play a role in making the justices little understood by the public. Chief Justice Warren at the time he took office considered supplementing the Court's annual statistical report to Congress with an assessment of its substantive decisions as well, a sort of backward-looking "state of the judicial union" message. He has apparently abandoned any such notions as further exposing the Court to the political pressures he seeks to counter. By and large, critics of the Supreme Court get no answer from the bench, except perhaps an occasional, usually veiled reference in a public address by an individual justice. Explanations, even of this sort, are not regarded as proper judicial etiquette.

On the whole too, the Court gets a bad press, not necessarily in the sense of an antagonistic one, but in the sense of inaccurate interpretation of its decisions. Newspapers and press services usually assign unprepared, run-of-the-mill reporters to the Court. The device of "decision Monday" means that a number of decisions, sometimes

[16] AIPO Poll, August 8, 1945, reported in H. Cantril and M. Strunk, *Public Opinion* 1935–1946 (Princeton: Princeton University Press, 1951), p. 39.

a half dozen or more on important matters, are all released at once; particularly toward the end of the term, when large numbers of opinions are finally read, reporters from the evening papers are hard pressed to digest the opinions. The mores of American journalism tend to favor hard-hitting headlines that all too often reflect misunderstanding by a local headline writer of the garbled version by a rewrite man of a story written under extreme pressure by an ill-prepared novice in legal matters.

Recently the newspapers have taken some steps to correct their problems. Anthony Lewis of the New York *Times* has been a leader in the improvement of legal journalism. Lewis took a year off from journalism to go to law school. He prepares himself elaborately before decisions are announced and writes carefully on major stories. He contributes to the law reviews and is highly regarded by the legal profession. James Clayton of the Washington *Post* is similarly careful and thoughtful and has achieved respect. The wire services are placing greater emphasis upon specialization. Yet reporters for evening papers still labor under extreme handicaps, and the Court itself, working against severe time pressures, has so far not found much merit in the notion of spacing out decisions. It sometimes alters the timing of a decision a trifle, but for its own convenience rather than for that of the reporters. The Court regards the use of official press releases as a public relations tool suggesting a quest for publicity not in keeping with the Court's role and dignity. On the whole, the Court seems justified in its refusal to accept such methods, for Chester Newland, who has extensively studied press coverage on Court matters, concludes that a large percentage of errors creep in at the local level, beyond the point where any of the reforms that have been suggested for the improvement of Court reporting would be helpful.[17]

Public response, of course, is not dependent upon interpretation of any single case, no matter how momentous. Rather, it is derived from the total impression made by the Court upon large numbers of people. "Image creation" is certainly an important element of the power of any institution dependent upon moral suasion. The absence of a regular Court constituency presents further difficulties for any Court representation to the general public. The one natural institutional support for the Court, the bar, is itself tied to diverse interests, largely finance and industry. The American Bar Association grew to eminence

---

[17] Chester Newland, "Press Coverage for the United States Supreme Court," **17** *Western Political Quarterly* (1964), pp. 15–36. I have drawn heavily from this source.

in the half-century subsequent to its foundation in 1889 as a firm supporter of a conservative Court. It has found it harder to embrace judicial review that develops doctrines generally opposed to those of the upper middle class and the business community, toward whom the bar's leaders are naturally inclined.

In any event, most lawyers themselves have little time for the Court and no exceptional understanding of constitutional issues. It is estimated that only a score or so of law professors and practitioners devote themselves to the study of constitutional law, always a step-child of the profession. When support for the Court has been forth-coming from the bar, it has characteristically been couched in the form of generalized appeals in the name of the rule of law. These are probably the most effective claims anyway; the justices have, how-ever, felt that the bar's support for the Court has been meager, with frequent criticism much more common. Major legal support tends to come from intellectual and university circles. The law reviews have been growing in number and stature and today are cited as authority by most courts in the land. While they also print articles critical of the Court, their general tenor is one of support for the institution and, on balance, for most of its decisions as well. Justice Frankfurter's strong connections in the legal world and the great respect in which his scholarship and teaching prior to his coming to the Court were held resulted in continued support for his point of view in the law reviews after he became a justice. It is a complex question as to which wing of the Court drew more encouragement from such articles, but Frank-furter himself was with the majority on many of the more contro-versial matters, particularly segregation, religious freedom, and a fair number of the criminal procedures problems. In any event, most law professors stand "Left of the Court's center" and certainly not hostile to the institution.

The principal political support for the Court today comes from the so-called lib-lab coalition: the loose, oftentimes warring coalition of labor minority groups, urban-based governmental agencies, free speech advocates, and defenders of individual freedom in the John Stuart Mill tradition. There is considerable overlap between this coalition and the Democratic party, though it is hardly the totality of the party, nor are Republicans strangers to the coalition. On some issues—national security versus individual freedom, and the church-state question, in particular—a great many of the members of this general coalition part company with Court defenders, while conserva-tive Republican leaders often will side with the Court majority. (It was, after all, Charles Evans Hughes who defended the New York socialist assemblyman and Douglas MacArthur who instituted great and far-reaching civil rights reforms in Japan.) Additionally, industrial and commercial interests rely heavily on judicial support generally, and with regard to such questions as interstate taxation upon the Supreme Court specifically. Nevertheless, the potent coalition functions most of the time and, because it is currently most effective in the executive branch and the Senate, is thus reflected as a key force in the Court as well.

However, constituency and pressure have rather less meaning for the justices than for other agencies of government. Accountability is largely institutional rather than personal when life tenure is involved. Professional and public opinion make their mark upon the Court, though to a lesser degree than where there is public control over actual tenure in office. The responsibilities of the justices thus remain essentially to their own consciences.

But the institutional accountability and the possibilities of a diminution of Court authority and Court respect remain real and enduring checks on the Court's self-assertion. In recent years the Court has, in the face of this, taken on grave responsibilities in the name of the creation of a "more perfect union," the achievement of a more democratic democracy. In so doing, it has made its own role even more anomalous; why an "inherently oligarchical" institution should prevail and should be uniquely trusted to defend majoritarian control has always been a question provoking learned gymnastics in the past. If time proves that the Court's efforts at statesmanship have provoked only additional confusion and problems, a diminution of its authority can certainly be expected as a consequence of the misunderstanding both of its own role and of the society of the future. Only the future and the American people can give the ultimate decision on the Supreme Court; it is in the scales of history that work of the justices will be weighed.

The nature of the fundamental relationship of the Court to the people remains an open question, unsettled even by the 1937 Court fight. As Justice Jackson has written:

> The country asked, "Is the judicial department or the will of the people supreme in America?" The Senate answered "Yes." The President had said, "Let younger men constitute the judicial department." The question was then left to another generation.[18]

[18] Robert Jackson, *The Struggle for Judicial Supremacy* (New York: Knopf, 1941), p. 195.